A LITTLE BOOK of LIGHT

sparks of hope,
moments of prayer

Alice Camille

TWENTY-THIRD PUBLICATIONS

twentythirdpublications.com

For my sister Evelyn, who has traveled
through the darkness and found the light.
With gratitude for sharing that light with me.

TWENTY-THIRD PUBLICATIONS
One Montauk Avenue, Suite 200
New London, CT 06320
(860) 437-3012 or (800) 321-0411
www.twentythirdpublications.com

The Scripture passages contained herein are from the New American Bible, revised edition © 2010, 1991, 1986, 1970 Confraternity of Christian Doctrine, Inc., Washington, DC. All rights reserved.

Cover photo: ©stock.adobe.com / kokotewan

ISBN: 978-1-62785-703-1
Printed in the U.S.A.

 A division of Bayard, Inc.

CONTENTS

INTRODUCTION

Story is home. Our stories are where we live and move and have our being. We come to know who we are in the context of where we've been, whom we've loved, and what's happened to us so far. Wherever we go, we take our stories with us. And wherever our stories go, we go along for the ride.

The 21st century has been a tough ride for many of us. I carry a happy verse from Isaiah in a ready mental pocket. It helps me through the rougher moments: "The people who walked in darkness have seen a great light" (Isaiah 9:1). Like so many others, and perhaps like you, I've known the darkness intimately. I also trust the great light with all my heart and soul. And, every once in a while, I find myself suddenly immersed in such radiant hours that my whole being is swallowed up in gratitude. The time spent traveling through the dark turns out not to be wasted. The hope in the unseen light proves to be more than just a dream.

Riding shotgun with Isaiah for so many years has taught me the importance of shared stories. Our sacred stories from Scripture have been passed along for two thousand years and more, reminding us all that the darkness we endure is temporary. The great light is still ahead, and we can get there from here—wherever *here* happens to be for you.

This book is an attempt to pass a candle of light along a little farther. It's divided into three sections of meditations that involve receiving the light, learning to trust it, and, finally, preparing to share it with others who could use some illumination. It's not the sort of book you have to read all at once. You can pick it up when needed and put it down when it's time for personal reflection. You can decide each day whether receiving, trusting, or sharing light is the task you're presently engaged in.

This is meant to be a comfortable, generous, and forgiving book! There are no "have to"s contained in these pages. You can look up the fuller Scripture passage connected to the citation if it's helpful. If you feel like praying, a starting line is offered. If you're a pragmatic person, a step to take is suggested. When the book has served its purpose for you, you might want to pass this candle of light to someone else.

Story is home. Our sacred stories are a home prepared to welcome us at any time we stop by. I hope you find a welcome in these pages and a place to call home. I'm leaving this light on for you.

RECEIVE
the LIGHT

Comedies of Salvation

"Are these all the sons you have?" Jesse replied, "There is still the youngest, but he is tending the sheep." 1 SAMUEL 16:11

We've done our best to separate religion from anything remotely fun. It can be tough to consider the Bible in terms of comedy. But this story is meant to tickle the funny bone. So, take a risk and smile at the scene being enacted here. Here's Samuel, an important prophet with a horn full of sacred oil, on a sacred mission to anoint a king. He comes to Jesse, who's flattered to host the prophet on such an errand. Jesse presents his seven sons, strong and tall and handsome. He's about to become the proud papa of Israel's king! What a great day for him and Mrs. Jesse.

Until Samuel rejects all seven and asks if there are more. More! Not many men can present seven sons. Luckily, Jesse has a spare kid in the back. He drags the smelly little boy out of the sheep pen. Thus, David's glorious reign begins.

Raise up for us, O Lord, leaders who are no strangers to the margins of society.

PAUSE AND CONSIDER: Do you know other stories of little people who became great leaders? How can you be a leader right where you are?

That Buzzing Sound

"Awake, O sleeper, and arise from the dead,
and Christ will give you light." EPHESIANS 5:14

Here's a comedy that is no joke. You and I are invited to fullness of life, happiness, and peace, the richness of God's bounty, for all eternity! This is our faith. Yet most of us slumber on, oblivious to the offer. You can hear the snoring from where you're sitting.

And maybe, just maybe, the snoring is coming from us. We spend many waking hours like sleepwalkers, moving through routines with eyes closed to the possibilities for greater, deeper life being held out in every moment. We could be serving the needs of the poor. We might love someone who needs to know that love is real. We're summoned this hour to kindness. Our forgiveness is required. *Zzzzzz.*

How will I live fully if I refuse to look, listen, feel, and act? How will I ever know if I don't stop what I'm doing, for just a moment, and let the silence of God penetrate me?

Wake me up, Lord of the dawn,
before I dream my life away on fantasies.

PAUSE AND CONSIDER: What methods do I use to anesthetize myself against fullness of life: food and drink, entertainment, crowds, remaining a moving target, avoiding solitude?

Fully Alive

"Why this commotion and weeping?
The child is not dead but asleep." MARK 5:39

"Resurrection" is a word that usually points in one direction: to the Easter mystery. But three additional stories of restored life appear in the gospels. The most dramatic concerns Lazarus, who answers the summons to come out of his tomb four days after he died. Yet he returns to the living without the slightest hint of the odor of decay clinging to him. It's as if death knew it wasn't his time. Another story of restored life involves the son of a widow in Nain. The widow's journey to the grave with her son's body is interrupted with the arrival of Jesus. Then death itself is interrupted. The final story concerns a twelve-year-old girl. On the cusp of fertility, she succumbs to a fatal illness. Then the promise of youth is returned to her. In each episode, Jesus insists that death is not God's will for us. God intends for us to be strikingly, stunningly alive.

Lord of life, thank you for the gift of time, and relationships, and resources.

PAUSE AND CONSIDER: Which aspects of your life seem "in the tomb" at this time? How might you be called from this grave?

Bear with Me

Preserve the unity of the spirit through the bond of peace. EPHESIANS 4:3

I still remember Susan. She came to our parish programs and wasn't an easy person to love. Defiance defined her persistently balled fists, her lifted chin, and her dispute of every teaching she heard. Sometimes she decried our "spineless" orthodoxy; at other times, our "offensive" pastoral generosity. It seemed she came only to fight. One day, Susan asked to speak with me after the session. I'd rather have been mauled by bears and thought of calling for backup. *Just love her*, I told myself. Predictably, she started yelling, while I stood with her and let her yell, keeping my heart and face soft. It went on for a small eternity. When she'd said it all and was quite empty, she started weeping. I caught and held her in my arms. After that day she never came back, but I think she got what she came for.

Lord, teach me how to love people who are hardest for me to love.

PAUSE AND CONSIDER: Have you ever tried to do what Paul says: bear with others in humility, gentleness, patience, and love, no matter what they do?

Where There's a Will, There's a Way

By endurance and by the encouragement of the scriptures we might have hope. ROMANS 15:4

By scientific estimates, humans have had hundreds of thousands of years on this planet. That's long enough to louse things up, but also time enough to get wise. Wisdom is available to anyone who seeks it. But it's not enough to buy a book of wisdom. You have to read it and take it to heart.

For believers, the Bible is such a book. It contains the inspired testimonies of people who learned (often the hard way) what it costs to walk in the way of truth. Yet for all the reverence paid to Scripture, few churchgoers actually read it. We may be intimidated, as we are of the arcane car owner's manual. Think again: the Bible is more familiar than that. It's the story of folks like us taking a journey toward home, family, community, and wholeness. If we want to know who we are, why we're here, where we're going, the Bible's one sure way to find out.

Guide me, Lord, to the intersection between my story and your Sacred Story.

PAUSE AND CONSIDER: Make an easy commitment to reading the Bible. Find a translation that attracts you and is easy to understand. Start with a verse a day. Highlight the ones that speak powerfully to you.

And They All Lived Happily

"Because this widow keeps bothering me I shall deliver a just decision for her." LUKE 18:5

In fairy tales, the weak are pitted against the strong. Yet the weak win. Red Riding Hood outsmarts the wolf. The lost children, Hansel and Gretel, defeat the witch. Against all odds, innocence overcomes malice. This makes for the classic happy ending. Unfortunately, it happens more in fairy tales than in real life.

Jesus goes beyond fairy tales in the story of the widow and the unjust judge. The judge doesn't reverse his verdict because it's the right thing to do, any more than the wolf decides Riding Hood and her grandmother are decent souls who shouldn't be molested. What defeats the judge is fear of retribution: he has nightmares about the widow coming after him with an Uzi! He resolves to escape the hassle and harm of dealing with her further. If a Big Bad Judge can be intimidated into justice, imagine dealing with God, who desires justice more than we do! No wonder we can anticipate a very happy ending.

Author of justice, strengthen our courage as we work to defend the weak and voiceless.

PAUSE AND CONSIDER: Who plays the role of the unjust judge in our society, and who plays the widow? How do you participate in the defense of those suffering from injustice?

Make Time for Wonder

"You also must be prepared, for at an hour you do not expect, the Son of Man will come." MATTHEW 24:44

I most surely did not expect to encounter Jesus that morning in front of the bookstore. I was in a hurry; the man in the wheelchair was blocking my way, waving a little plastic shopping bag and refusing to move out of the way until I looked inside it. Whatever he was selling, I knew I didn't want it. Whoever he was, I knew I didn't want an encounter with him!

But because he was persistent, I finally agreed to look into his shabby little sack. And there I found it: the full wonder of God. The bag contained reprints of some of the most amazing paintings I've ever seen. The man before me was an artist, half paralyzed and nearly speechless from stroke, forced to sell his art by sheer force of will. Who would have guessed that heaven was waiting in that crummy plastic bag? And I almost missed it.

God of Surprises, continue to confound me with your unexpected grace.

PAUSE AND CONSIDER: Make time where time is lacking. Take care where hearts are fragile. Seek beauty and expect miracles.

Behold the Mystery

*I resolved to know nothing while I was with you except
Jesus Christ, and him crucified.* 1 CORINTHIANS 2:2

Take a moment to catch your breath here, and witness a rare moment when Saint Paul is being humble! Paul is well educated for his times. His letters demonstrate great learning and deep thought. He wears the multiple hats of founder and theologian, preacher and teacher, arbiter and traffic cop. Yet with the Corinthians, who consider themselves cosmopolitan and sophisticated, Paul surrenders fancy rhetoric and sticks with the most basic theme of Christianity: Jesus and the cross.

This is the mystery Paul comes to reveal. Like any mystery, it remains partly concealed even in its revelation. Shine a light on the cross and it raises as many questions as it answers. The cross looks like the end of hope, the worst thing that could happen. Yet God made it a doorway to the best thing we can imagine. It was as confounding in first-century Corinth as it sounds today. And it's still the only gospel we need.

*I am full of words, and you are the Word.
Teach me to enter your silent Mystery.*

PAUSE AND CONSIDER: Sit before a crucifix. Contemplate the silence of God and the surrender of Jesus. Relinquish the need to understand, and open your heart to the mystery.

Seeing Is Believing

"You were born totally in sin, and are you trying to
teach us?" Then they threw him out. JOHN 9:34

Here is a story about the blind leading the blind, and just about everyone winds up in the ditch before the end—except the man born blind.

Consider the comic angles. The disciples pass a blind man and
wonder if it's true what people say: that blindness is a sign of sin. Jesus
denies the folklore and heals the man instead. The neighbors are so rat-
tled, they doubt this sighted guy is the same person they see daily. The
Pharisees, similarly shaken, question if healing comes from God or the
devil. The man's own parents are afraid to get involved. Meanwhile the
man, formerly known as blind, sees the whole thing quite clearly. He's
prepared to make a profession of faith. But not before he gets preachy
with the preachers, who promptly toss him out. Chances are they poured
themselves a stiff drink next. Maybe they even drank themselves blind.

God of truth, illuminate my path so
that I may not be left in the dark.

PAUSE AND CONSIDER: Look around at the ceiling or sky, at the floor
or ground. Catalog people, trees, furniture, wall hangings, dirty dishes,
whatever's there. Now close your eyes—and see more.

Joyful, Joyful, We Adore Thee

They ate their meals with exultation and sincerity
of heart, praising God. ACTS OF THE APOSTLES 2:46-47

When people talk about the good old days, it sounds too good to be
true. Did everything really cost a nickel? And no one had to lock their

cars or their homes? Were all families so close and cozy around the dinner table every night? Was there ever so much joy to go around?

Perhaps our memories are colored by the inescapable realities of the present. These days, a nickel is useless. Every bike has a lock. Families rarely have schedules that can accommodate a shared meal. Joy itself begins to seem antique, found only in the attics of the past.

But when we read about the joy known to the early Christians, we have to revise our pessimism. The word used to describe their experience is "exultation"—when was the last time you felt that? Exultation is the emotion of those who claim a victory. This victory belongs to all who believe.

Holy Spirit of God, help me to cultivate the spiritual fruit of joy.

PAUSE AND CONSIDER: Under what circumstances do you feel joy or exultation? Do you believe that Easter makes you, personally, a winner?

Indescribable Joy

You rejoice with an indescribable and glorious joy,
as you attain… the salvation of your souls. 1 PETER 1:8–9

We're attracted to smilers like moths to a flame. Julia Roberts' megawatt grin made her a fortune. People who smile get more votes, exude confidence, and are generally successful in whatever they do. It's as if they're in possession of a wonderful secret we'd all like to hear.

Another reason smiling people attract us is because joy seems so rare. Too many people are anxious, cranky, lonely, angry, depressed, bitter, cynical. In short, they fall into just about any category except happy. Where does real joy come from? How do we get there from here?

Joy is grounded in a peaceful heart, which comes from a life of confidence in God. Trusting in people (especially ourselves) never works, because people make mistakes; sometimes they betray; and always, sooner or later, they die. Only what's lasting can save us, and God is forever. Eternal joy: now there's something to smile about.

Lord, quiet my soul like a child at rest, that I may experience peace and joy in your protection.

PAUSE AND CONSIDER: Do you know someone who's genuinely joyful? What makes their heart so light and free?

Reasons to Hope

Unclean spirits, crying out in a loud voice, came out of many... and paralyzed and crippled people were cured. ACTS OF THE APOSTLES 8:7

We want to see this kind of power active in the world again. Too many are possessed by unclean spirits: drink or drugs, gluttony and consumerism, sexual objectification, the glorification of violence. Let's hear those spirits leave with a shriek, so that the tormented and deceived can be free. Their loved ones wait for that day.

We also long to see friends, bound by the effects of stroke, accidents, disease, and depression, lift up their heads and walk clear of their chains. It will be a joyful, holy day when they do. May hospitals and nursing homes be emptied and the streets full of dancing.

In the meantime, my friends, let us pray. For the church, to whom such power has been given through the Holy Spirit. Pray that we who are church will accept our spiritual gifts and exercise them in Jesus' name. Pray for courage and faith to fulfill the vocation to which we're each called.

Lord of hope, heal my afflictions and fears so that I may rise up and face another day.

PAUSE AND CONSIDER: Do you believe that the Holy Spirit has the power to heal you? How do you live out what you believe?

A Gift with Your Name on It

To each individual the manifestation of the Spirit is given for some benefit. 1 CORINTHIANS 12:7

The Spirit blows where it wills. Its gifts are planted everywhere, seemingly randomly, but according to God's purposes. We recite them in list form: Wisdom. Understanding. Knowledge. Right judgment. Courage. Reverence. Wonder and awe in God's presence. Here and there, the church is sown with this evidence of the Spirit at work in our midst.

These gifts raise up saints. John Vianney was known for wisdom in directing all who sought his help in confession. Katharine Drexel took understanding to a new level, insisting on providing Black and Native American children with the tools of a sound education. No one was more learned than Thomas Aquinas, no one as discerning as Catherine of Siena. Oscar Romero showed enormous courage in speaking the truth in the face of violence. Few have prayed like Teresa of Avila; few revel in God's creation like Francis of Assisi. And as the Spirit blows, the saints keep coming.

God of mercy, give this generation the saints it needs, and bring to life the saint in me.

PAUSE AND CONSIDER: Name people you know who illustrate the gifts of the Holy Spirit. Which of these gifts is coming to life in you?

Hearts on Fire

*Then [the need to speak in the LORD's name] is as if fire is
burning in my heart, imprisoned in my bones.* JEREMIAH 20:9

One of the most appealing aspects of Jeremiah's prophecies is that they
spring from a passionate heart. He conveys the entire gamut of human
feeling, from deep love to outrage, fear, depression, even disillusionment. More than any other prophet, Jeremiah is portrayed as a real
person with real weaknesses. He's one of us.

The name of God lives in this prophet's bones like a burning fire that
must be released. He reminds us of other fiery hearts mystically revealed
to us: the image of the Immaculate Heart of Mary first fostered by St.
John Eudes, or the Sacred Heart of Jesus that came to us by way of St.
Margaret Mary Alacoque, both of 17th-century France. These familiar
illustrations of hearts on fire demonstrate the Holy Spirit's passion that
sweeps over the church at Pentecost. The Spirit lights this same holy
flame in those who love God. Our hearts, too, can burn like this.

*Living fire of love, ignite my heart with
passion for justice, peace, and holiness.*

PAUSE AND CONSIDER: Is your heart on fire with the love of God?
Are you ready to spread that fire everywhere you go?

True, Lovely, Gracious

*If there is any excellence and if there is anything worthy
of praise, think about these things.* PHILIPPIANS 4:8

One traditional approach to morality has been to focus on the negative.

It's the "Thou Shalt Not" track, and it's older than the commandments. The Beatitudes of Jesus focus instead on the positive and represent a "Blessed Be" approach to encouraging goodness. Paul takes this route in focusing our attention on truth, beauty, and grace. Life has many pitfalls directing us to our own comfort and security. If we concentrate on them too long, even in the hope of avoiding them, we fall under their spell all the same.

Another worldly detour is toward cynicism and disillusionment. If we fall prey to it, we lose hope that people can ever be better than they are. We may begin to believe in the ugliness more than the wonder that also surrounds us. Dorothy Day noted that the world will be saved by beauty. Turn to the praiseworthy and lift up your heart!

In creation, in art, in invention, and in love, help me to see your face, O God of beauty.

PAUSE AND CONSIDER: Where is beauty present in your life? How often do you find a reason to praise?

Either Way, I'm Yours

I have learned the secret of being well fed and of going hungry, of living in abundance and of being in need. PHILIPPIANS 4:12

Mark Twain's *The Prince and the Pauper* is a well-loved children's story, widely imitated but never surpassed. We marvel at two quite different personages exchanging places, discovering the joys and miseries of the other's circumstances. Being a prince has its privileges, but also tedium and responsibility. A pauper's world can seem exhilaratingly free, but hardship and want are constricting. Both boys realize that neither situation is ideal and choose to return to the one they know best.

Saint Paul appreciates the experience of being both prince and pauper.

He learns the secret of being at peace in either circumstance. Mystics call this discovery the principle of detachment: since neither state is "who we are," both are external to our true identity in God. "Naked I came into the world, and naked I go again," as Job once learned. The lighter we travel, the easier we move in and out of need and plenty.

Compassionate God, rescue me in need,
and don't let me lose sight of you in bounty.

PAUSE AND CONSIDER: What kind of abundance do you enjoy: material, relational, intellectual? Where do you experience need? How can you practice detachment in both categories?

Small Steps, Big Results

"Since you were faithful in small matters, I will give you great responsibilities. Come, share your master's joy." MATTHEW 25:21

An elderly friend tells how she discovered her vocation. Forced to leave an abusive husband on short notice, she needed a new home for herself and her children, fast. The realtor had only one house in her scant price range: an abandoned crack house on the wrong side of town. The interior was painted in gaudy, violent colors: blood red, glow-in-the-dark green, black and white stripes creeping up the walls and wrapping all around the ceiling. In desperation, my friend agreed to take the house. She had one thought: to buy some paint and redeem those rooms! She'd never held a paintbrush and had no idea how to begin. But she learned. Painstakingly, from one room to the next, she learned by trial and error how to paint. So began her career as a professional housepainter, which provided for her family for 20 years. We can do nothing without taking the first step. God will return our smallest investment one hundredfold.

Lord, lead me on the path of wisdom and fruitfulness, no matter how unexpected.

PAUSE AND CONSIDER: When has an apparent detour in your life turned into a revelation? How has the person you are now come from small choices and even past mistakes?

It Happens

I myself will pasture my sheep; I myself will give them rest—oracle of the Lord GOD. EZEKIEL 34:15

Today, a high school boy finally expressed rage at his mother's death and broke the spell of depression. A man with a heart condition agreed to begin a weight-loss program. A woman realized she can't control her drinking. Two people who normally engaged in casual liaisons decided their new relationship was too important to treat with irreverence. A pregnant single mother of two decided to seek adoption for her third baby rather than terminate its life.

A couple on the verge of divorce sought counseling instead. Brothers who hadn't spoken for years because of something neither could rightly remember had lunch together. A burned-out teacher spoke to the principal about taking time off. A father forgave his daughter for not being the child he'd expected. The girl forgave her father for expectations that had constrained her for years. And so, God continues to rescue the flock, wherever they're scattered, and leads them home.

Lord of the lost, keep your eye on all of your wandering children.

PAUSE AND CONSIDER: When have you been lost and needed a shepherd to lead you back? Who or what helped you find your way home?

This Is Your Personal Invitation

*May the God of peace… make you perfectly holy and may
you… be preserved blameless.* 1 THESSALONIANS 5:23

Two words stump most of us mortals: "perfect" and "holy." Except for
the true megalomaniacs among us, most of us know we're not perfect.
And most of us don't think of ourselves as particularly sanctified. So,
when Saint Paul prays that we be made "perfectly holy," we mumble,
"Oh sure. Right." It sounds suspiciously like Mom telling you to sit up
straight.

We're right to assume our mortality can't be perfected. By biblical
definition, our humanity is subject to the effects of original sin. Still,
holiness is available to us. Holiness means participating in the life of
God, something we're asked to do regularly: our sacraments are signs
of this invitation. God's life is good—radically so. To share in that life
is to take small steps (and sometimes full plunges) into the practice of
goodness, love, and compassion. So, sit up straight, and stop being a
spiritual slouch! Get holy.

*Lord, may your sacraments guide me in the way
of welcome, mercy, service, and shared life.*

PAUSE AND CONSIDER: Name three holy things you've done this week.
Name three more you might do next week—and then do them.

Your Light Has Come

*Arise! Shine, for your light has come, the glory
of the LORD has dawned upon you.* ISAIAH 60:1

When was the last time you saw something you hadn't seen before?

Maybe you woke up in a new city, greeting unfamiliar walls that will one day feel like home. Or you walked into a new school or workplace that held fresh challenges and opportunities. New relationships, or fresh starts with old ones, can seem like virgin territory.

Each new situation holds an epiphany. It reveals something we can't anticipate or imagine from this side of the future. An epiphany is a twinkling manifestation of God, a glimpse of the divine face, sometimes just a wink between God and us to be sure we share the joke. It turns on a light so we recognize what we first knew only in abstraction, the way we see shapes in a dark room before flipping the switch. God doesn't mean for us to be left in the dark. Happily, the route between God and us is well lit by epiphanies.

We love the familiar and the well-worn. Yet, Lord, you make yourself known in the new.

PAUSE AND CONSIDER: Look for epiphanies of God's love and beauty in the world. Resolve to become an epiphany of God's love for those around you.

The Rescue Continues

The mystery of Christ… was not made known to human beings in other generations as it has now been revealed. EPHESIANS 3:4–5

We come to know the God we serve within the journey we take. That's why we speak of salvation *history*: there is, properly speaking, no mere "saving moment" but a long evolution into the realization that God has been saving us all the while. Through many divine rescues from the time of Noah, Abraham, Moses, and Mary, gradually we become aware that God doesn't only save certain folks now and then but intends to rescue the world one suffering soul at a time.

Salvation comes in the form of an ark, a promise, a liberator, and a Word made flesh, to name just a few manifestations. Trust that there'll be more to come. Along with the universal signs of our rescue—bread and wine, water and oil—there are private ones, little miracles we come to know as daily bread and friendship. The mystery's not known to anyone else the way it is now revealed to you.

Sometimes I need a lot of saving, and other times just a little. Lord, be my safety always.

PAUSE AND CONSIDER: List moments of salvation history as you know them from the Bible. Follow them across the route they've taken in your life. How are they alike, and how are they different?

Reverence

And the lord whom you seek will come suddenly to his temple. MALACHI 3:1

"Elvis is in the room!" my friend announces when he wants us to rise and greet an honored guest. It works. We'll all rise for "Elvis." As the 19th-century essayist Charles Lamb once noted, we'd rise for the likes of Shakespeare: "But if Jesus Christ should come in, we would all kneel." In the person of Jesus, the standard of awe is at a magnitude beyond mere celebrity.

The Holy Presence is unmistakable. Walking into an empty church, we're hushed by our awareness of the sacred, the palpable sense of generations of prayer and worshipers, the communion of saints, kingdom coming. We may have that same awareness in the sight of natural wonders or at the hour when hope is fulfilled or love is made real. Malachi describes the divine encounter as a purifying experience, purging away all that's not "good as gold" within us. When our hearts are on fire, it's time to get down on our knees.

*Lord of all creation, give me the spirit of
reverence like a burning, purging fire.*

PAUSE AND CONSIDER: In what places or circumstances are you aware
of the presence of holiness? How do you respond to that awareness?

Between Beasts and Angels

*[Jesus] was among wild beasts [in the desert],
and the angels ministered to him.* MARK 1:13

In the scheme of things, we often find ourselves somewhere between
the beasts and the angels. Like the beasts, we're bound by the limits of
mortality. We're subject to need, error, weakness, suffering, and death.
Yet we're also like the angels: we have a higher destiny and orientation
toward God. We experience both postures in the restless longing for
more. As Saint Augustine put it, "You have made us for Yourself, O
Lord, and our heart is restless until it rests in You."

Our sacred story can hardly be told without beasts and angels. Noah
relied on a dove, ravens attended Elijah, Balaam had his ass, and Tobias
his trusty dog. Jesus rode into Jerusalem on a donkey. Meanwhile,
angels employed Jacob's ladder and stepped into history often to confer
with Abraham and Isaiah, Zechariah, Mary, and Peter, to name a few.
Let's celebrate our place in the blessed chain of creation!

*Lord of the animals and angels, open my eyes
to the way all creation ministers in your name.*

PAUSE AND CONSIDER: Consider the contribution of the natural
world, and the heavenly one, to your present life. Who has been an
"angel of grace" for you?

Sitting in the Dark

The light came into the world, but people
preferred darkness to light. JOHN 3:19

Imagine someone entering a room lit by a single lamp at its center. Yet she chooses to sit in the darkest corner. What might this tell you about that person? She is tired, perhaps, and wants to shut her eyes. The chairs at the room's edges may be more inviting. Maybe she's shy, nervous, or doesn't want to be engaged. Maybe she's ashamed or has something to hide.

We can imagine all kinds of reasons why people choose the world's darkness over Christ's light. They may prefer to shut their eyes to what sounds like weary work and thankless obligation. The world may seem to be a more attractive place to get comfortable. Fears and anxieties of many kinds keep people from engaging religion. Guilt can keep them at a distance, or the sense they wouldn't be welcome because of who they are. Meanwhile, Christ's compassion, forgiveness, and inclusive love offer an incandescent invitation.

Source of wisdom, lead me to seek your light
and to illumine the way for others.

PAUSE AND CONSIDER: The light of Christ burns for you. Light a candle and contemplate the relationship of light to darkness. Pray for someone lost in the dark.

Being Human

"The author of life you put to death, but God raised him from the dead." ACTS OF THE APOSTLES 3:15

Name three things about being human that delight you. I'll tell you mine: the vivid painted colors on my little niece's fingernails that she did "all by herself." Listening to Art Garfunkel sing of pain so delicately in "Bridge over Trouble Water." The caress of silk.

We could also name more troubling things. How easily fear tempts us to be cruel. The way age adds aches and removes dexterity. The certainty that those we love, no matter how we protect them, can be hurt.

Jesus is born fully human. He was of Abraham's line, a son of David, born of Mary. Surely he had a favorite color, fragrances that delighted him, words that moved him deeply. We know he wept at the blindness of Jerusalem and chafed at the cowardice of his followers. Yet he is also "author of life" and divine Son. He could be murdered, but his presence could never be extinguished.

God of infinite mystery, how wonderful that you choose to be one with us.

PAUSE AND CONSIDER: Contemplate your favorite image of Jesus. What does it reveal of his humanity? What does it tell you of the divine life he shares with his Father?

Something So Great

*"Ask now of the days of old, before your time… : Did anything
so great ever happen before?"* DEUTERONOMY 4:32

What impresses you most about God? Okay, since I raised the question, I'll answer it too: ever since I was a kid, I've been delighted with the size and strength of God's SILENCE. I grew up in a multigenerational household, where clamor and crowds were the order of the day. I loved visiting empty churches during the week and listening to God's silence. The vastness and cavernous echoes in those churches were part of that experience: to this day I mix up "hallow" and "hollow" in my mind. God is so big and important and busy, I'd imagine, yet manages to get everything done QUIETLY, without leaving a trace.

Yet Moses is most impressed by the opposite attribute: God's ROAR. God performs many technicolor saving acts on behalf of Israel—burning bush, assorted plagues, Red Sea parting. That's a lot of holy hoopla. Whatever you need, soft or loud, trust God to supply it.

*God of profound words and deep silences, teach
me to be more aware of your movement.*

PAUSE AND CONSIDER: Name three times you were aware of God's action in your life. What characteristics of God are revealed in these three?

In Heaven, the Lame Man Dances

*Then the lame shall leap like a stag,
and the mute tongue sing for joy.* ISAIAH 35:6

My brother spent his last months in a wheelchair. The tumor in his brain confounded his speech until he was reduced nearly to silence.

When he tried to make himself understood, it caused anxiety all around. The words that came out were not the words he intended. No one knew what meaning was locked inside him.

The last time I visited him, we sat together in frustrating silence. Not wanting to prolong it, I started humming a familiar hymn. My brother joined in, note for note, in perfect pitch. The trouble in his speech didn't affect his capacity to find the music. Overjoyed to have found a shared language, we sang together one hymn after another: I sang the words and my brother used whatever words became available to him. In music, we'd discovered a communion the angels must enjoy in God's presence, glorious and full. I wonder if heaven will be like that, with nothing standing between us all.

Lord, make my heart like the psalmist's, who found true spiritual communion in songs.

PAUSE AND CONSIDER: Sing. Listen to sacred songs. Let instrumental music take you to the place beyond words. Find celestial harmony in the power of music.

God's Word Is Alive

The word of God is living and effective, sharper than any two-edged sword. HEBREWS 4:12

Revelation tells us the word of God is the ultimate wisdom. Still, I went to church every Sunday and didn't open the Bible personally until I was in my 20s. I didn't get what all the fuss was about. I knew the stories. I heard them in church. Was I missing something, not reading Scripture for myself?

Eventually, I surrendered. I committed to reading three verses a day, and I was pretty faithful for about a year before noticing any effect.

I wasn't exactly making a dazzling commitment of time, to be sure: television was getting a LOT more of my attention than the Bible. Yet sheer exposure counts for something. They say the Grand Canyon's vastness doesn't open to you until you look at it for a long, long time. There came an hour when my perspective expanded. Suddenly I knew the Word had taken root in me and was beginning to grow. The word of God really is alive!

Every day I'm bombarded by stories that sow death. Make me attentive to stories that give life.

PAUSE AND CONSIDER: How much time do you surrender daily to opening junk mail or watching commercials? Are you willing to give as much time daily to a holy word?

More than the Light

Beyond health and beauty I loved [Wisdom], And I chose to have her rather than the light. WISDOM 7:10

Name your greatest desire. What would you be willing to do to acquire it? The writer of the book of Wisdom prayed for the spirit to be wise. More than power or wealth, health or personal attraction, wisdom was his pearl of great price. As he observed, light only has splendor while it's shining. Wisdom's radiance never sleeps. Why settle for a lesser brilliance?

Yet most of us do. How many people do you know who've made it their personal quest to attain wisdom? Is your list as short as mine? Most folks have more worldly goals, even if they're religious-minded. Many simply hope to make it through the day or to the cocktail hour. Achieving wisdom would seem meaningless within such an agenda. Wisdom's path transforms our perspective, broadens our horizons, and changes what we value and seek. Only those willing to be changed will seek such a prize.

Source of wisdom, my ignorance has been costly.
Make me willing to pay the price to be wise.

PAUSE AND CONSIDER: List people you know or have read about who seem truly wise. What price did they pay to acquire this prize?

Here Comes Wonder

Nations shall walk by your light, kings by the radiance of your
dawning. Raise your eyes and look about. ISAIAH 60:3-4

Would you know wonder if you saw it? The prophet Isaiah does—but remember, he's not talking about something visible to the eyes. He speaks of a vision for the future, not the way things look in his generation. His present is no more radiant than ours. Yet he's capable of seeing beyond grim realities to what could be.

How about us? Can we see splendor beyond the brokenness and peace past all the violence? Do we dare imagine a world better than the one we know or a future different from the past? It's easy to get trapped by "reality," resigned to how things are, as if we were bereft of options. We trust more in sin than in salvation. After all, sin has crouched on the lion's share of human history, while salvation seems to appear in rare cameos. Such cynicism has no place among the faithful. It's the visionaries who speak for God.

Master of time and eternity, help me to
remember that the future is in your hands.

PAUSE AND CONSIDER: Can you trust in a thing you can't see, even more than in what appears before your eyes?

The Alphabet of Grace

The Gentiles are coheirs… and copartners in the promise in Christ Jesus. EPHESIANS 3:6

What's a revelation? It's more than insight and much more than a conclusion we can arrive at by adding up the facts. Logic moves us from A to B and arrives at C. But if you move from A to B and come up with a new alphabet entirely, that privileged perspective is more in line with the idea of revelation. Prophets and saints often contemplated the events of their day and gazed through them to the future that God had in mind. Since folks around them were stubbornly adding up the logic of the situation and arriving at a more obvious future, they thought the seers were crazy.

Paul's revelation—that all people are potential partners in God's plan of salvation—sounded ludicrous to those accustomed to writing off whole categories of persons. Still determined to arrive at C, they refused to entertain the new alphabet of grace.

*Teach me a new language, God of hope,
so I can speak your message of inclusion.*

PAUSE AND CONSIDER: We're socialized to think in terms of insiders and outsiders, winners and losers. God embraces everyone and hopes we all become winners.

Reading the Signs

I will place a sign among them; from them I will send survivors to [those] which have never... seen my glory. ISAIAH 66:19

A 1971 song by the Five Man Electrical Band called "Signs" made sport of posted warnings. "Do this" and "don't do that" remain simple bits of advice that are good to follow. Still, we often miss signs provided for our well-being. We're pretty good at obeying blatant ones like STOP and YIELD, painted in hard-to-miss colors. But when "STOP" and "YIELD" aren't spelled out so plainly, do we discern the urgency of the warning? Sometimes, the alcoholic will put down her glass and know it's time to stop for good. The enraged person may recognize he's already said too much and elect to shut up. Yet decades of warnings didn't prevent dramatic climate change, a worldwide season of sickness, or the church sexual abuse scandal. Meanwhile, God continues to post signs furiously through human history and our personal histories to guide us in our choices. Once in a while, we take the time to read them.

Lord, you send us prophets and sages in every age to tell us the truth. Help us to hear it!

PAUSE AND CONSIDER: What signs have you read in time to keep you from making poor choices? What signs might you have refused to read until it was too late to prevent disaster?

Faith Wanted

*The vision is a witness… a testimony to the end; it will not
disappoint. If it delays, wait for it.* HABAKKUK 2:3

Did you have an early dream for your life, for your child, or for the
way the world should be? Maybe you wanted to be a superhero, ath-
lete, great artist, or saint. Time and experience tend to erode our early
dreams and make us into fatalists. We start to expect less from life and
less from ourselves as we gradually submit to "the way things are" and
"the way the world works."

Yet some folks manage to hang onto their dreams and make them
come true. Why should cynicism, which colors the world in dark tones,
be a more truthful way of seeing the world than idealism, which bathes
the same world in radiant light? The only way to remain an idealist is to
practice the virtue of faith: in God, in the ultimate goodness of God's
creation, and in the power of love as stronger than evil, stronger even
than death.

*Creator of all things, you have yet to give
up on the world. Strengthen my hope!*

PAUSE AND CONSIDER: How would you describe God's vision for the
world as expressed in the Bible? What has to change for that vision to
become reality? How must you change to participate in that vision?

Rise and Shine!

"Awake, O sleeper, and arise from the dead,
and Christ will give you light." EPHESIANS 5:14

Most of us prefer a cleaner distinction between "sleep" and "death" than Saint Paul is making. Still, unconscious is unconscious: either we're paying attention and are fully awake or we're as good as dead. Either we chase the lie of popular culture that life is about making money and acquiring power or we're awake to our true identity as the free and blessed children of God. Either we assemble relationships to benefit ourselves or relate to others with a concern for what's good for them. Either we dwell in the darkness of taking what we want or are growing in the light of peace, justice, and mercy. And if light is our choice, then Christ will give it to us. Christ shines a light into the world's darkness so we can see how things really are. If clarity appeals to you, all you have to do is wake up and step into the light.

Lord of light, awaken me in the midst of daily routines to see what you would have me do.

PAUSE AND CONSIDER: Which aspects of your life seem "awake" to spiritual realities, and which are still "asleep"?

Rest Assured

"Come to me, all you who labor and are burdened,
and I will give you rest." MATTHEW 11:28

My friend was a drinker. The kind who lost jobs, broke hearts, destroyed relationships, and woke up in strange places he couldn't remember arriving at to begin with. His life thrilled with romance, tragedy, and pain, and he didn't know how to make the Ferris wheel of passion and doom stop. Until the day he showed up at Mass, of all places, after decades of absence. The gospel that day happened to be this one. He heard Jesus speak directly to his heart: "Come to me, all you who labor and are burdened, and I will give you rest."

The burden my friend was carrying was heavy. It was crushing him. The idea of rest made tears start from his eyes. Would Jesus really carry this burden for him? Would the yoke Jesus laid on his shoulders be sweeter to endure? In that moment, he resolved to put his burden down. And as promised, Jesus took it up.

Lord, make me as committed to being healed as I've been to being in pain.

PAUSE AND CONSIDER: Take this to heart: it all doesn't depend on you and your efforts. Lay your burdens down at the foot of the cross and find the rest Jesus desires to give you.

Tend Your Garden

"Let [the weeds and the wheat] grow together until harvest." MATTHEW 13:30

Someone said that weeds are just flowers you haven't learned to love. I have both weeds and flowers in my garden. I'm fairly ruthless about pulling up the weeds I recognize: the ones that attract undesirable bugs or produce thorny things that stick to my socks. The ones I don't recognize I allow to grow for a while. I let them demonstrate what they're capable of. Maybe they're not so bad. Or maybe they are. Time always tells.

People also need time to show us what they're capable of. First impressions can be way off. Even bad actors can become better people over time. I hope I'm a better person than I was 20 years ago. Maybe a little better than last year, even. I try to learn from my mistakes and learn more from the mercy shown to me. God is good. I am much less so; but I'm not quite as bad as I used to be.

Gardener of my soul, teach me to discern between what belongs and what doesn't.

PAUSE AND CONSIDER: When has a weed in your life turned out to be a flower in disguise?

TRUST
the LIGHT

The Promise in History's Haystack

A shoot shall sprout from the stump of Jesse,
and from his roots a bud shall blossom. ISAIAH 11:1

Remember when you were young and Christmas morning took forever to arrive? For grownups, it's a blink of an eye between one year and the next. Even as time rushes by with age, progress remains sluggish. Each generation knows war, famine and sickness, social upheaval and horror. Every heart endures loneliness, loss, and regret. What gives us reason for hope?

Israel's hope concerns the "forever kingdom" that was supposed to descend from King David's household. Yet four hundred years after David, Babylonian exile put an end to that hope. The line of David's father, Jesse, was leveled like a tree stump. By the time of Jesus, King Herod is on the throne: a puppet ruler humored by Rome. Generations had waited for the promise to be fulfilled, for a king to make Israel great again. Could that leveled stump bloom again? The seer Isaiah promises that it will.

Loving God, you believe in me even when I don't believe in myself. Help me to embrace hope.

PAUSE AND CONSIDER: Name one way you look to the future with hope. Name one way you would change the past if you could. What step can you take today to start fresh?

ID-ing the Messiah

"The one who is coming after me is mightier than I." MATTHEW 3:11

Someone regularly emerges on the world stage claiming to be the rescuer we've been waiting for.

Many of John the Baptist's followers saw him that way and were filled with the hope of deliverance. Was John the messiah of their longing? Or was he Elijah, returned to anoint a new "forever king"? John had Elijah's wild look about him. His message was equally stark, critical, and commanding. Hearts raced as he spoke.

John is clear that he's not the one people are waiting for. He's just as firm in predicting the approach of hope. The past was dark. John urges people to renounce the old way through baptism. To prepare for hope's arrival, they must free themselves from yesterday's despair. As Mother Teresa would say 20 centuries later, even God cannot fill what is full. If we empty ourselves of the old disappointment, we'll have room for new life. So: what are we waiting for?

Dear Lord, give us wisdom to make healthy and holy decisions as we travel forward.

PAUSE AND CONSIDER: Make room for hope. Seek the sacrament of reconciliation. Make peace with those you've injured or who have caused you injury. Clear space for prayer, silence, and change.

Fear Is Useless

God did not give us a spirit of cowardice but rather of power and love and self-control. **2 TIMOTHY 1:7**

If God didn't give us fear, where does it come from? Its spirit is alive and well in the hearts of many. Fear keeps us from becoming who we were born to be: the free children of God. Cowardice teaches us that the way of safety is by means of financial security and social acceptability. It means sacrificing our moral code and private dreams, sometimes even our families, to the engines of material success. In the end, we may seem powerful. But everyone knows the schoolyard bully is the biggest coward of all.

Genuine power comes from divine authority, which needs no wealth or coercion to back it up. Godly power expresses itself in the persuasive manner of love and the mastery of self. It takes moral courage to control ourselves and to surrender to the love of God and others. Fear can't hide in the presence of love.

Lord of boldness, cast out fear and raise up heroic hearts in your name!

PAUSE AND CONSIDER: What are you most afraid of? How does the love of God and those around you offer you a way out of fear?

Unchained Melody

Naaman's flesh became again like the flesh of a little child, and he was clean [of his leprosy]. **2 KINGS 5:14**

Success is nothing if you harbor a great despair. Naaman was a valiant general, but what good is the respect of your king if you shrank from loving your wife? What good to command an army if you're ashamed of your own body? Leprosy was a broad term describing infirmities ranging from the merely disfiguring to the life-threatening. Whatever Naaman suffered was enough to drive him to a foreign prophet in search of a cure. Anyone with miserable adolescent acne or who spends night after night crawling with eczema can sympathize.

Seven plunges in the Jordan later, Naaman's a free man. Imagine his astonishment, pleasure, and rippling laughter as he runs his hands over his new skin, the old misery gone for good! From now on, he wants only one God, the One whose prophet knew how to make a suffering man like a child again.

You create us to be both free and responsible.
Help us to find the balance in our stewardship.

PAUSE AND CONSIDER: What keeps you from experiencing greater liberty? How does God invite you to wash yourself clean of the past?

What Did You Go Out to See?

The wilderness and the parched land will exult....
Be strong, do not fear! ISAIAH 35:1, 4

In a world in which the news is often dreadful, how wonderful it is to get good news. In the prophetic world of Scripture as well, the news was routinely alarming: *The world will be destroyed by flood! Your city will be leveled by fire!* So, when Isaiah brings a message of hope and consolation, there's cause for celebration. The desert blooms. The feeble are made strong. The frightened have no reason to fear. I want to live in that realm!

When will this time of endless celebration come? When will those who have suffered physical and emotional losses be restored? This is the real message of incarnation: not that we're waiting for a babe to be placed in a manger but that the time of restoration is really at hand. Bad news may arrive by the hour; yet the news, ultimately, is good. The courage to believe in hopeful outcomes is called faith.

Thy kingdom come, Lord, and thy benevolent will be done.

PAUSE AND CONSIDER: Are you a pessimist or an optimist? Cynical or hopeful? How does your faith shape the way you receive the daily news?

Life in the Cheap Seats

God chose the lowly and despised... those who count for nothing, to reduce to nothing those who are something. 1 CORINTHIANS 1:28

A lot is made of the saying "The poor you will have with you always." Some of it is frankly awful theology. Jesus doesn't suggest that we accept poverty as a permanent fixture on the social landscape. Yet here, Paul suggests that God repurposes our injustice for divine ends. Since God prefers all things to work toward the good, the lowly might provide an object lesson for the proud.

Here's how it works. The powerful rely on themselves because— well, because they can! A poor choice, since trust is rightly placed only in the Lord. The powerless, meanwhile, rely on God because God is all they have. The strong would be wise to follow their example. In the same way, those who count for nothing in the grand scheme of things give glory to God, while those who are celebrities now take glory for themselves. Here again, the lowly might supply lessons in humility.

Lord of the small and humble, teach me to place all my trust in you.

PAUSE AND CONSIDER: Under what circumstances do you place your trust in God, and when do you prefer to rely on your own resources?

Bringing Out the Dead

You shall know that I am the LORD, when I open your graves and make you come up out of them, my people! EZEKIEL 37:13

It doesn't matter who you are, where you live, or what you've got. The kind of car you drive won't make a difference. You may have a lot of money or owe a lot of money. You can have a PhD or a GED. Your hair may be black, gray, or hard to find these days. No matter the details of your life, the end result is the same. We're going to die. Really. No kidding.

That doesn't mean we should just give up and watch television. Or eat, drink, and be merry. Death is serious, but so are the claims of Christianity. The resurrection confirms what ancient prophecy hoped for: that death, though it's the end of life, will not be the end of us. Do you believe this? If you do, it should color who you are, how you live, and what you do with what you've got. If you don't believe it, of course, there's always TV.

Lord of life, into your gracious hands I place my trust.

PAUSE AND CONSIDER: Do you believe in the resurrection of Jesus and your own resurrection? How does faith in eternal life make a difference in the present life?

Love Wins

"This illness is not to end in death, but is for the glory of God." JOHN 11:4

Jesus said the illness wouldn't end in death, but it did. Lazarus died. And so have our friends and loved ones over the years, some of them great believers in the promises of Jesus. We've known people who've prayed and prayed that their cancer would go away or the doctors would find a cure for their child in time. And when death arrives anyway, it hurts terribly: for those who have to let go of the life they know and for the ones who have to say goodbye too soon.

Lazarus dies and his family grieves. Even Jesus weeps out loud at the loss of a friend. But then, Lazarus is restored to their midst! And now we understand what Jesus meant: not that Lazarus wouldn't die but that death wouldn't be the end of him. Death may win the battle, but love wins the war. So we believe. So we profess.

Source of my being, I believe that you have the power to lift us up to life everlasting.

PAUSE AND CONSIDER: Pray for the dead. Remember them in the Eucharist and recall that they are part of the communion of saints, present in the assembly of the faithful. Live in hope.

My Yoke Is Easy

For whenever anyone bears the pain of unjust suffering because of consciousness of God, that is a grace. 1 PETER 2:19

Beware any religious instruction you get—even from me!—about patient suffering. Too much unnecessary suffering is passed off by well-meaning people as "good for you" when it clearly isn't. Any child knows hurt is to be avoided whenever possible. But many an adult shoulders suffering with a sigh, calls it "a cross," and refuses to put it down even when given the chance. This is frankly unhealthy, to fall in love with misery.

To learn more about the kind of suffering that really is redemptive, contemplate the cross of Jesus. He didn't want it. He prays passionately in the garden to be relieved of this burden. But human hatred and the love of God made the cross unavoidable. Jesus embraces the sacrifice that true love demands. Being human promises us each an unavoidable share in suffering. Faith teaches us how to accept it with grace and humility. Let the rest fall away.

God, help me to bear the suffering that cannot be avoided and to lighten the load for others.

PAUSE AND CONSIDER: When has unavoidable suffering come into your life? What can you do with such suffering through the power of grace?

Love Speaks

"The sheep hear his voice, as [the shepherd] calls his own sheep by name and leads them out." JOHN 10:3

Listen. The voice of love is calling you. The Beloved calls us by name and we can't resist the sound.

Think of the voices you find irresistible. Perhaps it's your child calling from another room. Maybe it's your spouse, parent, friend, or someone who depends on you for care. A friend of mine once needed me this way and grew too ill to call out. We set a bell near his bed so he could ring, night or day, for help. At first I found the mid-night ringing wearisome. It meant getting out of a warm bed to do something difficult. But soon I came to hear it as the sound of love calling. Then it became a summons to tenderness I was glad to hear.

In the voices that call for us, we hear the greater call to charity, which has God as its ultimate end. Listen! God calls you into the arms of love. Wherever you hear that voice, surrender your heart.

You who speak to prophets with a whispering sound, teach my heart to hear and respond.

PAUSE AND CONSIDER: Recommit to responding to the voice of love. Resolve to make your reply with generosity rather than impatience. Remember: the voice you hear is the Lord's.

The Power of the Wind

When Jesus had said this, he breathed on them and said to them, "Receive the holy Spirit." JOHN 20:22

One night a windstorm wrecked my garden. It was just a little second-story balcony garden of potted flowers, but it was all I had. Plastic pots flew overboard, rolling so far down the street they were never found. Terracotta pots were dashed to pieces, broken branches of much-loved plants strewn pathetically in a sea of mud. It was a sad morning, requiring a stiff upper lip and an attitude adjustment.

When the Spirit blows through our lives, things will change. It can feel like a destructive energy. Indeed, some things may have to die for new ones to be born. Shortly after my garden was demolished, I was offered a job in another city. I was freer to make the move without the plants.

Though the Spirit may also come as a gentle breath, as it does in the episode with Jesus and the disciples, that can be deceptive. Hidden in that soft breath is still the full force of Pentecost. Those disciples are in for some changes.

All-powerful God, we praise you for the many gifts you give to those who trust in you.

PAUSE AND CONSIDER: Pray the prayer of enlightenment: Come, Holy Spirit, fill the hearts of your faithful. And kindle in them the fire of your love. Send forth your Spirit and they shall be created. And you will renew the face of the earth.

Do Come Along!

"If I find favor with you, Lord, come along in our company.... Pardon our wickedness and sins, and claim us as your own." EXODUS 34:9

What a marvelous prayer Moses prays! He acknowledges the moral messiness of the people yet offers them to God as they are. Then he invites God to walk with them, sins and all. Rather than offering an unblemished lamb, it is the troublesome, ambiguous, defective human heart he offers. And God accepts.

Why would God want the companionship of human beings, who come with a limited warranty for very good reasons? I don't know about you, but people drive me wild sometimes. We, however, have no choice: we're social creatures, dependent on each other in ways both bothersome and wondrous. Whereas God, in splendid and self-sufficient Trinity, exists without need of more. Still, God, inscrutably, chooses relationship with us. All I can say is, it's a good thing for the human race that I'm not God. I'd build a beach house on the Baja and you'd be on your own!

Merciful God, thank you for your generous willingness to walk with the likes of me.

PAUSE AND CONSIDER: Do you have the courage to offer God your heart with all its imperfections? Or the compassion to accept other people with all of their imperfections?

Show a Little Guts

"Please, Lord, for even the dogs eat the scraps that fall from the table of their masters." MATTHEW 15:27

Even dogs can hope! This is what the woman says as she asks Jesus to heal her tormented daughter. She classifies her Canaanite family with the dogs, knowing most Israelites would do the same. Jesus approves her faith and gives her what she desires.

Some claim Jesus was testing her by not responding immediately to her request. Others say Jesus learned from her to enlarge his mission beyond Israel. It's intriguing to consider that any one of us might summon up the courage to tell Jesus how to run his own ministry. Many prophets and saints showed this kind of spirit, sparring with God over matters that were vital to them. Who knows what could happen if more people prayed with such confidence? Who knows how many of us might dicker, wrestle, and argue with God—like Abraham, Jacob, Hannah, and the Canaanite woman—and win?

Gracious God, do I trust you enough to show you my heart?

PAUSE AND CONSIDER: Show some chutzpah! Resolve to pray for the things that are most important to you: peace on earth or with your spouse. Don't let go without a blessing.

You Called Me?

"You are Simon the son of John; you will be called Cephas" (which is translated Peter). JOHN 1:42

Simon becomes Peter. Saul becomes Paul. And further back, Abram morphs into Abraham, Sarai into Sarah. Jacob becomes Israel. We have to ask: What's up with this? The permanence of names was clearly not assumed in ancient cultures.

One thing the Jewish community was always firm about is human wholeness. When you change, everything changes: your heart, behavior, clothes, right down to your name. Half measures were unacceptable. The new name is a constant reminder that you can't go back to who you were and the life you lived before. This practice is continued through the taking of a new name in religious life, at Confirmation, and sometimes in marriage. Still, the experience of being called out of your old life and into a radically new identity is something maybe only spies, movie stars, and gang members appreciate fully in our modern culture. If you could be someone radically new, who would it be?

Lord God, when you call me, make it loud and obvious so I can't mistake it for anyone else.

PAUSE AND CONSIDER: Listen for the new identity God may be calling you to assume. It can be a secret name you share with no one else: Beloved. Servant. Champion. Kindness Bearer.

The Kingdom Is Now

"This is the time of fulfillment. The kingdom of God is at hand. Repent, and believe in the gospel." MARK 1:15

We can't count on empires, and we can't count on our own strength. So, either we wind up as frightened children or we find someplace else to put our trust. Jesus spoke of a time of fulfillment in which all hopes come to flower, not to ruin. He called this era the kingdom, but make no mistake: this is no earthly empire. Our kingdoms are places on the map, showplaces of human achievement. God's kingdom isn't a place; it's a time. According to Jesus, that time is now.

If the kingdom is now, how do we get to "now"? Jesus replies: Change direction and have faith. Direction is important since most of us are oriented toward the past or future. We dwell in old disappointments or mistakes or in future plans that may never be realized. To live in the kingdom, we have to abandon what is not and reside fully in this hour. God is here. The kingdom awaits.

Patient God, I live so quantumly: leaping from past to future. Hold me in the now!

PAUSE AND CONSIDER: Practice kingdom living. Do what you can in this hour, in the place you are, with the people given to you and the gifts you have.

God's Generous YES

For however many are the promises of God, their
Yes is in [Jesus Christ]. 2 CORINTHIANS 1:20

We're used to a realm of red lights and green lights, of permissions granted and denied, of yes and no handed down from a higher authority. Even in our happiest hours, we may wait for rain to fall on the party. Childhood memories are sown with disappointments: the day the kite string broke, someone important forgot a birthday, or a promise wasn't kept. Cynicism begins here.

We have to unlearn that attitude in our relationship with God. Others may earn our mistrust because it's human to fall short and to fail. God isn't subject to limitation. Divine promises do not disappoint. Their fulfillment is on view in the life of Jesus, who is God's Yes writ large across history. Yes, there's forgiveness for the most desperate sinner. And freedom from despair, and life beyond death. There's healing, hope, and restoration from the worst we can imagine. The cross is God's Yes raised high above our darkest hour.

God of the promise, I place all my trust
in your care and protection.

PAUSE AND CONSIDER: Name an experience in your life that felt like a denial or red light to your happiness. How does God's Yes in the person of Jesus answer that denial with hope?

I Do

*I will betroth you to me forever... with justice and with
judgment, with loyalty and with compassion.* HOSEA 2:21

I was recently transfixed at the wedding of a friend. I've known Elaine
for years as a coworker, pal, and polka partner. (Believe me, when
you've danced the polka with someone, it takes the relationship to
another level.) As I watched Elaine come down the aisle with her
espoused, I saw a transfigured woman. Surely the formal dress and pro-
cessional music added to the effect. But what was most startling was the
sense of purpose and focus in Elaine that I had not seen before. Her
life seemed gathered into that moment, crystallized and covenanted.
She was choosing each step with great deliberation. I saw more than a
woman on her wedding day. I saw a wholeness that amazed me.

God seeks this for us: a gathering of everything we've been and have
yet to be, offered in joy for the single-minded purpose of living in love
forever. Wholeness, and holiness, are not far apart.

*In baptism, Lord, I committed my way to you.
Make my every step purposeful and true.*

PAUSE AND CONSIDER: When have you felt a clear sense of purpose
and direction in your life? How is such wholeness related to holiness?

Who's in Charge?

*I will raise up shepherds... who will shepherd them so that
they need no longer fear or be terrified.* JEREMIAH 23:4

We suffer from a lack of capable leaders. Politicians follow the money.
The nation follows its appetites. Our children follow celebrities. Often

our heroes are long dead—or entire fictions from movies or TV. Those who lead wisely are few, and the possibility of their corruption is ever present. Even among church leaders, you may be hard pressed to name many who've proven responsible in your lifetime.

If you've had good mentors, thank them. If you've had wise teachers, appreciate them. If your political representatives have integrity, support them. If family members inspired you to follow a higher calling in life, celebrate them. And if anyone looks to you for guidance, share with them the blessings you've received. Without leadership, many will go missing from the flock, lost on a path with no cairns or guideposts. If no one in your vicinity is leading, it may be a sign that your leadership is required.

All authority originates in you, Lord, and all powers must bow to your holy name.

PAUSE AND CONSIDER: Name folks in various categories who've proven their ability to lead well: in government, church, society, or your family. What characteristics mark a worthy leader?

Far Away, So Close

In Christ Jesus you who once were far off have become near by the blood of Christ. EPHESIANS 2:13

The best stories involve heroes who rise up from humble means, fight insurmountable odds, and manage to beat them. That's the appeal of fairy tales—Cinderella, Hansel and Gretel—not to mention Harry Potter and Hermione, or Frodo and Sam. Historical figures we admire share this backstory: Moses began as the child of slaves and later governs a people. Lincoln was born in a log cabin and becomes president. Cesar Chavez, a migrant worker, founded a movement to better the lives of farm workers. When the highly unlikely becomes reality, that's the essence of a good story.

Salvation history is the same kind of story. God gathers the unlikely (wayward souls like us), shepherds them through insurmountable obstacles (sin and death), and brings them to a remarkable result (redemption and eternal life.) For those who thought, "No way," there's now a way. Jesus is the Way. There's no better story than this one.

Jesus, lead me on your way.
Step by step, and hour by hour.

PAUSE AND CONSIDER: Which obstacles seemed insurmountable in your life—until you beat them?

Lost and Found

His heart was moved with pity for them, for they
were like sheep without a shepherd. MARK 6:34

Jesus is not about to lose you. No way. No matter how far you wander and where you wind up, Jesus is prepared to lead you back. It doesn't matter if you've neglected church, been married a few times, or done things that cause gasps in religious circles. You may have broken a few hearts—most particularly your own. Jesus has trailed you the whole while, and he's not prepared to give you up.

We sometimes imagine we've crossed a line beyond which God's compassion can't find us. God won't enter this darkness for us. Even the divine patience must have limits. But that's fear talking. And it's prideful to think our ability to sin is stronger than God's willingness to forgive. If you're within the sound of this gospel, know that Jesus always waits for you to follow him on the journey back to grace. The only thing that stands between God and us, generally speaking, is us.

There is nowhere I can go, loving God,
where you aren't ready to lead me home to you.

PAUSE AND CONSIDER: What are the things you find hardest to forgive in yourself? In others? Trust that God is up to the task of pardoning all of this and more.

Famous Last Words

My servant, the just one, shall justify the many,
their iniquity he shall bear. ISAIAH 53:11

When Father Ed was dying, he joked about how he was paying for his sins. Father Ed had cancer, yet he smoked cigarettes for as long as he could still hold one. Toward the end, he left his oxygen tent several times daily to light one up. He sent me to buy them for him by the carton. My heart was heavy on this errand, but a man in his 70s ought to be able to make his own decisions.

Father Ed was among the holiest people I knew. Though he joked about suffering being the price of his choices, he also spoke earnestly about the mercy of God he'd always counted on, especially now. God had forgiven him decades of hard drinking followed by years of grateful sobriety. God had blessed his wild years with protection and the season of peace with spiritual gifts. Father Ed accepted life and death on God's terms. God had accepted Ed on his terms too.

Lord, you transform sin into redemption and
suffering into grace. Rescue me from my choices.

PAUSE AND CONSIDER: How has your own suffering taught you lessons you couldn't learn any other way?

No One Given to Me Will Be Lost

At that time your people shall escape, everyone who
is found written in the book. DANIEL 12:1

Many say the age of the book has passed. The future's online; who
needs the printed page? Tomorrow's libraries may be largely replaced
by the Internet. Newspapers are already delivered electronically to
many homes. Future forests won't be sacrificed to our bookshelves.
After all, "written in stone" was once a literal reference to how media
was printed: carved in rock. The written form continues to evolve.

The idea of the book nonetheless remains the same. It's a place of
documentation, in its own way sacred and final. When I was a kid,
looking up a word in the dictionary resolved many arguments around
the dinner table. Webster got the last word! For people of faith, the
Bible enjoys this same vote-or-veto authority. In Daniel's prophecy,
the image of a Book of Life reveals the permanent commitment God
makes to us. Once recorded, our names aren't forgotten, and our fate
is assured.

Consecrated at baptism, named again at
Confirmation, you know my name, Lord.

PAUSE AND CONSIDER: What gets written down for posterity in your
home? Is the family tree recorded in a Bible? Do you keep a diary, jour-
nal, or blog? How does writing something down enhance its meaning?

Little Questions, Big Answers

His dominion is an everlasting dominion
that shall not pass away. DANIEL 7:14

Prophets often have dreams and visions that reveal cosmic truths in rich detail. The visions aren't necessarily literal, but usually highly symbolic. Even Jesus' image of the "kingdom" is a metaphor. The deeper reality Jesus evokes is the primacy of God's sovereignty. It's God's world, in other words: God alone is in charge. God is Lord of time and governor of eternity. All worldly authorities to which we submit in life won't be around forever: parents, bosses, domineering personalities. In the end, it will be just as God says in the First Commandment: You shall have no other gods before me.

It might be best to get used to following that commandment now, since it's the one and final rule for eternity. If there are powers that oppress or consume your life, don't give them your heart. You belong to a much higher power. It's God's world. Other claimants are just pretenders.

Liberating God, you rescue us from sin and death and from every tiny tyrant too.

PAUSE AND CONSIDER: What powers (like addiction, depression, parental expectation, peer pressure, economic demands) exert authority over your freedom? How can you find liberty?

Star of Wonder

"Where is the newborn king of the Jews?
We saw his star at its rising." MATTHEW 2:2

Signs and wonders were nothing new to the magi who followed the star. We call them wise men, philosophers, astronomers, even kings. More than anything, they were seekers of truth. Most people didn't look into the heavens to see what could be read there of God's designs. Most folks stayed home, attended to their business, and didn't go traipsing across deserts following a cosmic sign of a newborn king. Even if such a king had been born—so what? Why worship the latest in the seemingly endless line of royals?

These wise ones saw something unprecedented that stirred in them the desire to press forward into the unknown. Those on a quest can't explain to those who stay put why such a journey is necessary. Only those on the journey feel the tug and know the futility of resisting. To those who follow a star alone belong wonder and revelation.

When I'm most comfortable where I am, Lord,
move me out into new territory of growth.

PAUSE AND CONSIDER: Open yourself to wonder. Consider an unexplored route in your faith experience: a deeper commitment to prayer, daily Mass attendance, spiritual direction, a weekend retreat.

Take the Blessing and Run!

Blessed are those who trust in the LORD;
the LORD will be their trust. JEREMIAH 17:7

A friend of mine admits he doesn't want anything to do with religion. He considers himself an agnostic: skeptical of a God who cannot be seen or proved. My friend prefers to put his faith in science because it's something he feels sure of. Yet, I point out, gravity is invisible. Many scientific theories must be adjusted or even rejected as new evidence comes to light. I note that my friend believes in many things that can't be proven: his daughter's love, the safety of his money in the bank, and our friendship, to name a few. All of these things are like the realms of both science and faith: they can only be concluded by results they achieve or harvests they produce. Trusting in God is often dismissed as a metaphysical risk. Yet by all evidence amassed so far, trusting in material things and error-prone people is definitely a bigger risk.

Thank you, Lord, for all of the unseen things that make my life possible today.

PAUSE AND CONSIDER: Count the number of invisible things you rely on every day. The air you breathe. The care of loved ones. The arrival of the next moment.

Home Sweet Home

Our citizenship is in heaven, and from it we also await
a savior, the Lord Jesus Christ. PHILIPPIANS 3:20

Whenever I'm moving from one address to another, the place I'm leaving suddenly becomes unbelievably dear. I start remembering how warm my neighbors are, how great the public transit is, how delicious the food tastes in familiar haunts. The new address, by comparison, seems blank and ungenerous, offering nothing but risk. Divesting in one place and investing in another seems a great challenge. Still, before too long, the new address presents its possibilities. I start calling it "home" before I'm aware of having switched allegiances.

We're all heavily invested in the world we know. How could we not be? This world is home. But it isn't the only world in which we hold citizenship. Nor is the present hour all there is. The future awaits, and so does a realm beyond this one for which we're preparing. We may feel unsure about surrendering what's familiar for what lies ahead. But wait till we're there!

I believe you are the Lord of heaven and earth.
I may change addresses but not allegiances.

PAUSE AND CONSIDER: What steps do you take to claim citizenship in heaven while still investing in your present address?

It's Almost Here!

The expectation of your people was the salvation
of the righteous and the destruction of their foes. WISDOM 18:7

Are you waiting for anything? Does anticipation play a role in your life? Much of the time, we anticipate only the mundane: Friday, payday, or simply that hour of the day when we finally get to put up our feet. But now and then, time takes on a whole new significance as we count down the days until a particular event takes place: a visit from a significant person, a long-planned vacation, the day that movie we've been hoping to see is finally released. At these times, anticipation fills us with excitement and restlessness. We want time to pass quickly until the event arrives—

and then we pray time stands still as we savor our happiness. The book of Wisdom reminds us that God's people waited in Egypt seemingly forever for the night of their freedom to arrive. They believed in its coming, and they prepared to act as a free people the moment it was realized.

Source of Eternal Hope, we await each encounter with you as an episode of grace and joy.

PAUSE AND CONSIDER: Consider those things you live in anticipation of: holidays, encounters with people you love, special events. How do you prepare for their arrival?

Flowers in the Desert

The wilderness and the parched land will exult…
it shall bloom abundantly. ISAIAH 35:1–2

A cactus flower is a visual paradox. It grows on a prickly, drought-ridden plant without an inch of softness to it. A careful hiker avoids it at all cost. And yet, come spring, this spiny, unfriendly creature puts forth the most delicate, colorful blossoms imaginable. Its petals are like tissue paper, the palette as varied as any painter's. A cactus flower looks like some rare bloom achieved under pampered conditions. But it pops out untended by any gardener in barren territory.

To desert people, a cactus flower becomes a sign of the surprising and unearned goodness of God. Isaiah uses the image of a blooming desert not because it's miraculous and rare but because it's miraculously predictable without losing any of its wonder. Just as delicate flowers bloom in deserts, so does God bring healing and freedom to those who trust the divine promise. If you've ever seen a cactus flower, you know nothing is impossible with God.

Lord of surprises, train my heart to be confident that your promises are true.

PAUSE AND CONSIDER: Wonderful things come from surprising directions. Kindness is offered from an unlikely source. Resolve to bring beauty to places where it's lacking.

Finding Favor

[God] called us to a holy life, not according to our works but according to… grace bestowed on us in Christ Jesus. 2 TIMOTHY 1:9

It's vanity to believe God might be attracted to us or bless us because of our personal goodness. Before time began, Scripture says, we were called to a holy life—imagine, long before we were born! God's grace has been available and operative for our sake through all eternity. You and I have been on God's mind for a very, very long time.

So, if you've lived a totally virtuous life up to now, congratulations and best wishes for your future canonization. And if you've made some bad choices and have some things to be sorry for, like me, God is still calling you to holiness from time immemorial, and that hasn't changed. And if you've *really* botched things up so far—and maybe wrecked a few other people as collateral damage—there's still hope. It's not according to our deeds, but according to God's amazing grace, that you and I are rescued.

Generous God, you don't play favorites; you love all of us as though there were only one of us.

PAUSE AND CONSIDER: Does it sound like good news or bad news that the worst sinner and most virtuous person can both be redeemed by God's grace?

Death Isn't Terminal

Thus says the Lord GOD: *Look! I am going
to open your graves.* EZEKIEL 37:12

We all know folks who've risen from the dead. Not in the creepy, horror movie sense but through the normal course of navigating a world fraught with failure and loss. Some survive the train wreck of divorce and go on to love again. Some experience the death of a dear one so acutely, they lose seasons to recovery before they're able to rejoin the living. Some die to their old abilities and sense of self as they grapple with disease and disability. Some return from the grave of addiction; others, from aimless habits or misdirected goals.

All of these deaths are places from which God can rescue those who seek restoration. God also provides a way out of the big death, too— the one formerly known as final. If we find ourselves among the living dead now and again, we're guaranteed one thing: it's not God's will for us to be there. God's will is always and urgently directed toward life.

*Living God, you will us all to fullness of life.
Rescue me from every shadow of death.*

PAUSE AND CONSIDER: What kinds of deaths have you already passed through? How was that "grave" opened?

Entering the Mystery

*Mary of Magdala came to the tomb early in the morning, while
it was still dark, and saw the stone removed.* JOHN 20:1

When we approach a mystery in the dark, as Mary did, we may not see more than a tomb ajar. This tells us nothing. Vandals may have been here. Or disciples hoping to create a legend. Enemies may intend to stir up scandal. An open tomb is ambiguous when viewed in the dark.

Another disciple arrives on the scene with Peter. It's now dawn. At the tomb they can see a little better. The unnamed disciple peers in but remains at the entrance. He's not prepared to enter. From where he stands, he sees burial cloths but no body. At a distance, he's filled with confusion.

Peter enters the tomb. From within, he sees more: not just the burial cloths themselves, but how they've been thoughtfully placed. Who would uncover a body before stealing it? Hope emerges. This could be good. This could be very good. Entering a mystery is the only way to gain this view.

God of purposeful mysteries, reveal to us what we need to see to make our faith strong.

PAUSE AND CONSIDER: In what moments of your spiritual life have you consciously felt yourself entering the mystery in a deeper way? What did you see?

Sin Abounds; So Does Grace

Not one [sparrow] falls to the ground without your Father's knowledge. Even all the hairs of your head are counted. MATTHEW 10:29–30

A glance out the window confirms the world is full of sparrows. Sweep the floor and acknowledge how many hairs fall daily. Does God really keep track of each bird and strand of hair, along with ants, amoebas, and cells sloughed off in the shower? I don't doubt God can; I just marvel that God would lavish such care on each aspect of creation. Yet why not? If God took the time to fashion the amazing molecule H_2O

that we know as water, which turned barren dust into the soil of all life, why wouldn't God keep an eye on the microcosm?

Sin gets into every crevice of creation. We see its effects, so we have no trouble believing in sin. Even folks who don't believe in grace rarely doubt the existence of evil. Still, grace follows sin down every crack. The God of your lost hair and the hope of every bird isn't absent from one inch of history.

Gracious God, you accompany each atom on its journey. Give me reverence for your creation.

PAUSE AND CONSIDER: Imagine a season of your life when God seemed most absent and sin most powerful. Now imagine Jesus with you in that time, very close by. What does he say to you in that hour?

Pray Better, Not Harder

The Spirit too comes to the aid of our weakness;
for we do not know how to pray as we ought. ROMANS 8:26

Thirty years ago, I was hurt as badly as I've ever been hurt. What made it worse is that the person who injured me showed no remorse or concern for my suffering. I had recourse to the law. I knew I could sue. I thought long and hard about it. I spent five months, in fact, thinking day and night about justice, retribution, revenge, and what it might cost to feel good about my life again.

What I really wanted was to take back the past and make things as they were before. That, I concluded, was an impossible goal. I couldn't have my life restored the way it was. But I could have what God wanted for me right now: healing, wholeness, and hope restored. The only way to get those things was to offer that same possibility to the person who'd hurt me. After five months of crying and praying, I was ready to do that.

Healing God, touch my wounds and make them serve your holy purposes.

PAUSE AND CONSIDER: Do you come to prayer to talk or to listen? Do you pray to change God's mind or to be changed?

SHARE
the LIGHT

Ode to Light

*"You are the light of the world. A city set
on a mountain cannot be hidden."* MATTHEW 5:14

Light is for sharing. Alone, it loses its meaning: imagine the sun without planets, or green plants needing photosynthesis, or creatures to look up and admire the twinkle of a distant star. A light left on in a closed closet is of no use to anybody (except perhaps the electric company!). Light begs to be shared.

We set up lights around us for reading, for guidance down a dark hall, for atmosphere, and maybe that one cute little lamp just for beauty's sake. Light helps us celebrate: think Christmas trees, fireworks, birthday candles. We even leave a light on for people we love to remind them they're welcomed and anticipated. Light is purposeful, communal, inviting.

And for all these reasons, Jesus reminds us we're called to be light. Our testimony of kindness, mercy, and welcome illumines the way for countless others—some we know and some we'll never know. Being light, you might say, is our vocation.

*Source of all light, guide us in the way of being
light for a world content with darkness.*

PAUSE AND CONSIDER: Celebrate light. Watch a sunset or sunrise. Light a candle and pray for someone. Rearrange the lamps and see what new things come to light. Share the light with someone who needs it.

More than Enough

"Gather the fragments left over, so that nothing will be wasted." JOHN 6:12

Always we have fragments left over. No matter how scarce our resources are, there are bottles and paper to recycle and plastic bags to be returned to the supermarket. There are clothes in our closets we never wear, books we won't read again, gadgets that take up room and gather dust but serve no purpose. There are extra dollars to buy a lottery ticket or an ice cream. No matter how busy we are, there are hours to waste watching television, while relationships are squandered for lack of our attention. During my last move, I gave away one-third of my clothes because the new closets were smaller than the old ones. I never missed a single blouse or slipper from that pile. I could probably put half my life out on the curb and not miss a stick of it; eat half of what's on the plate and still be well fed. It would be terrible if we drowned in abundance, still believing we never got enough.

Generous God, thank you for everything I have. And loosen my grip on it.

PAUSE AND CONSIDER: What do you need to give away most right now: love, time, money, possessions?

Room for One More

And when they had eaten, there was some left over,
according to the word of the LORD. 2 KINGS 4:44

At a recent family wedding, a distant cousin showed up unexpected-ly, luggage in hand, without a hotel reservation. The extended family looked at him blankly, reluctant to take up the responsibility for one more person to house, feed, and ferry around on this busy weekend. Wouldn't you know it, the poorest member of our clan, the one with the least to share, grabbed the cousin's bags and offered him her couch. It reminded me again that to the generous soul, there's always some-thing to share. Often, we look at the bottom line of the checkbook during a charity drive and feel sure there's hardly enough for our needs. The doorbell rings at suppertime and it seems impossible to set a place for one more. But if we write the check, get another chair, we find that it's more than possible. For the generous, the jar of flour never goes empty.

Change my heart, O God, so that I'm eager
to share what I have in the hour of need.

PAUSE AND CONSIDER: When have you been the recipient of unlikely generosity?

Love Unending

They all ate and were satisfied, and they picked up the fragments
left over—twelve wicker baskets full. MATTHEW 14:20

Nobody goes hungry when Jesus sets the table. In fact, expect leftovers! This story is key to understanding our Eucharist. At the Table of the

Lord, there is no need. At the table Jesus prepares with his own life, there's always enough to share.

And so, we take the leftovers on the road, and I don't mean simply taking communion to the sick and homebound. We share Christ's life by comforting the hurting or sitting with the lonely. We share it with those hungry for hope or thirsty for justice. We are Christ's presence as we bring healing, forgiveness, compassion, and peace. And as we celebrate with the joyful, mourn with the sorrowful, or share the indignation of the poor, we set the table for more of God's people. The miracle of loaves and fishes is far from over. This meal is being multiplied and served wherever you go.

Food of the poor, alert me to the needs of those around me, that I might share your table.

PAUSE AND CONSIDER: When have you been served from the heart of Christ by a friend, family member, or stranger? When have you carried Christ to someone else?

Powers that Be

There was a strong and violent wind rending the mountains and crushing rocks... but the LORD was not in the wind. 1 KINGS 19:11

Where might we look for God? The prophet Elijah waited out a storm, earthquake, and fire in anticipation of the Holy. He recognized God in a tiny whispering sound. Yet today, "acts of God" are deemed catastrophic events. We hardly consider the God fully present in a bobbing wildflower or infirm relative. We expect God to be BIG. We forget the Lord who arrived in this world as a needy baby.

Can we find God in a pile of dirty dishes, signifying God's abundance? Do we see God in the sullen teenager, anticipating condemnation but needing acceptance? May we look for God in the irritating person, the luxurious shade on a hot day, or even the task that seems like a burden? God is almighty but also omnipresent: revealed all around and at all times. If we practice long enough we may, like Elijah, sense God in the most surprising moments of our lives.

God Almighty and Lord of littleness,
help me to seek and find you in all things.

PAUSE AND CONSIDER: Give five pieces of evidence that you have seen God today.

You from around Here?

"You shall not oppress or afflict a resident alien, for you were once aliens residing in the land of Egypt." EXODUS 22:20

Thirteen congregations of Catholic sisters in the Midwest pooled their resources to buy billboard time. They issued this invitation to passersby: "Welcome the immigrant YOU once were!" Few of us are native to this place. There's no moral ground on which to stand if we discriminate against the latest newcomers.

We have to make room for others in many ways: in our complicated lives, in the expansion of our families, and in our hearts. We make room for differences as we seek to understand what seems foreign or strange. We can't afford to close doors or to build fences too high.

The Christian writer of Hebrews, who is unknown, added an idea to the Exodus quote presently under consideration: "For here we have no lasting city, but we seek the one that is to come" (Hebrews 13:14).

Truthfully, we're all alien here, just passing through on our way home. How could we cling to a bit of ground, an hour, or a sense of who doesn't belong?

Lord God, to you no one is a stranger, and no one doesn't belong. Teach me your welcome!

PAUSE AND CONSIDER: How do you welcome the stranger, the newcomer, or the loner? How do you make room for others in your conversation and at your table?

Prepare the Way

Every valley shall be lifted up, every mountain and hill made low. ISAIAH 40:4

Every Sunday afternoon at five o'clock, my neighbor plays Handel's "Messiah" on her stereo. I should say she blares it, throwing open her windows and pouring the whole concert out into the air and through the neighborhood. This is not just a seasonal thing at Advent and Easter. She does it 52 Sundays a year.

And if it were any other kind of music, I'd probably protest. But how can you protest the "Messiah"? Each time, it makes me stop and recall what I'm doing here on earth, what my life is for, and who I say I'm waiting for. Winter, spring, summer, and fall, we Christians are vigilant for the Beloved who is eternally on the way. This arrival is so extraordinary that all of creation paves the way for it. Valleys shall rise up, hills shall bow low. And how shall we prepare the way? Shall we rise in holiness, bow in humility?

*O God, I'm exalted in bearing your
image and humbled by my injustices.
Smooth the path that leads to you.*

PAUSE AND CONSIDER: What aspects of your life might require lifting up to prepare for the Lord? What elements might need to be brought low?

Where God Lives

*The revelation of the mystery kept secret for long ages…
[is] now made known to all nations.* ROMANS 16:25–26

Where does God live? Children may point to the sky and say, "Heaven." Some of us might acknowledge the divine Presence in the tabernacle, the human heart, or the juxtaposition of justice and peace. Believers claim God is everywhere; atheists insist God is nowhere. But Christians unanimously declare that once in history, we knew precisely where God could be found. This manifestation of divinity, Jesus Christ, lived in an occupied country, part of an oppressed people, largely unknown and unimportant.

And Jesus told us to keep looking for him among the lowly. if we're looking for God's house today, it might be a hogan on a Native American reservation or in a barrio of Mexico. God might be in an apartment project in our cities or in a tent in a refugee camp. God dwells on a farm in China and in a hut in Africa. Wherever the little ones are, God reveals the divine mystery there.

*Champion of the poor, direct me to
opportunities to sacrifice and to serve.*

PAUSE AND CONSIDER: How do you see God in the disadvantaged? How do you love and serve God there?

Lopsided Holy Card

The Lord sets a father in honor over his children,
and confirms a mother's authority over her sons. SIRACH 3:2

The Holy Family is often presented as a model to emulate: noble father, immaculate mother, divine child. Frankly, there aren't too many families that match this description. Most families are more like the bread of our Eucharist: blessed, broken, and shared as they are. In our fractured reality of family, there's something consecrated nonetheless that speaks of God and goodness. Our Eucharist teaches us that the whole of divinity is contained within the tiniest piece. So, we might accept that even in the most fractured of families, wholeness and holiness can be found.

Sirach lists the mutual responsibilities of parents and children in an idealized version of family. Maybe yours is like that, and you can appreciate his advice. But if you came from a messy, mixed-up home like most people I know, find a way to honor that place and those people. Let the memory be blessed and made whole in you.

In all the ways my family is broken, Lord, help
me find your consecration through the cracks.

PAUSE AND CONSIDER: In what ways does holiness reside in your family? How does the brokenness of family consecrate you for the role you play now?

Wherever You Go, Bring the Light

They were overjoyed at seeing the star,
and on entering the house they saw the child
with Mary his mother. MATTHEW 2:10–11

When my youngest sister had her first baby, she received the gift of a wall hanging that proclaimed: "Babies are like stars. Each one shines with its own special light." This schmaltzy saying was accompanied by an appropriately sentimental illustration. Yet when I first looked down at my latest niece, so free of the imprint of time and care that grownup faces have, I saw that unique star shining through her perfect skin. The light of innocence can be blinding.

This same light once shone through you and me. Although dimmed by years and circumstances, it's still there, capable of guiding others to the light of Christ we follow. Jesus calls us the light of the world too. It's an awesome responsibility, yet as natural as the light glowing under a baby's skin. While time has colored us with many experiences, we can be stained glass, those colors adding to the brilliance and uniqueness of our witness.

Make me a moon reflective of your eternal sun, Lord, and let there be light!

PAUSE AND CONSIDER: Who have you known who bore an appealing light into your life? Is there someone you know who seeks such a light from you?

Words Made Flesh

*You are our letter, written on our hearts, known
and read by all.* 2 CORINTHIANS 3:2

We call Jesus the divine Word made flesh. We, too, are incarnate words spoken into the lives of others, for better or for worse. What words might be scrawled at the center of our being and imposed on those who know us? What do they hear when pressed to our hearts and permitted our confidence? Is it a word of hope or despair; expectation or cynicism; love or bitterness?

My friend Beryl lost her beloved husband after a difficult illness. Visiting her, I was braced to share her sorrow, anticipating loss without comfort. How astonished I was to find her bathed in the recognition of blessing and hope! The love she'd shared with her husband was strongly present. Her sadness was blended with so many beautiful memories. The word she bore most profoundly on her heart was "grateful." It was the word I carried away from our encounter: a deep gratitude for her testimony to a love stronger than death.

*Gracious God, thank you for the word you
write so eloquently across history: forgiven.*

PAUSE AND CONSIDER: Identify a word that might characterize the person you offer to the world today. What words are offered in the people around you?

Here Comes the Groom

*"As long as [the wedding guests] have the bridegroom
with them they cannot fast."* MARK 2:19

At modern weddings, outsized attention is focused on the bride. Every camera is aimed at her and the environment constructed around her: wardrobes, flowers, and more. Jesus focuses on the significance of the groom, equally central to the matrimonial event. His presence is reason to celebrate, his absence cause for fasting.

So let me say a few words about my friend Dick. He's an older man with a broken first marriage behind him and lots of sorrow to go with it. I don't think Dick expected any more happiness in life; and then he met Yoshiko. At their wedding, when Yoshiko approached him in the traditional Japanese kimono, most people were focused on this elegant woman in exotic clothing. I, however, was stunned by Dick, his eyes full of beauty and his whole body poised for the acceptance of fresh hope and a second chance. In the presence of such love, who could fail to rejoice?

Lord of second chances, help me to overcome fear and doubt and entertain new possibilities.

PAUSE AND CONSIDER: God's love comes to us with open arms and everlasting promises. Take a chance and open your heart, despite past disappointments, and embrace hope.

The God of Flesh and Bones

*"Touch me and see, because a ghost does not have flesh
and bones as you can see I have."* LUKE 24:39

The God of flesh and bones is a shattering revelation. We're pretty contented dualists: God's in his heaven, which is fine with us in the world far below. We spiritualize religious truths to the point of unreality. Religion happens in hallowed spaces and involves things that go up: incense, prayers, the flames of candles. What stays below—relationships, work, laundry, and bill paying—can seem outside God's jurisdiction or concern.

Yet God shows up in our territory, bounds into the room, asks for something to eat. We can be forgiven for being startled. God doesn't BELONG here. This world is for the mundane, pragmatic, and functional. It's also the repository of sin and suffering and tremendous dissatisfaction. It's not always pretty here, and having God show up at the door is frankly uncomfortable. There's no time to fluff the pillows and straighten up the mess. Yet all God wants, really, is to share a meal with us.

*At your table, God of abundance, we find food
for our hunger, the satisfaction of our thirst.*

PAUSE AND CONSIDER: Name three ways you can share a meal with the God of flesh and bones. When have you last shared such a meal?

The Nature of Greatness

Let us see whether [the just one's] words be true;
let us find out what will happen to him. WISDOM 2:17

In religion class, greatness often seemed defined as the willingness to die an exotic death for the faith. Shot full of arrows, nailed to a cross upside down, your head served on a platter, or other grisly martyrdoms were how truly great saints distinguished themselves. Much as I hoped to be a saint back then, the optional avenues weren't attractive.

Happily, the paths to sanctity are wider than originally proposed. God champions those who are just, not merely the exotically executed. While justice may require facing down one's opponents to the death, it's not the end that God prefers. The way of justice can be lived as well as died: in fair and loving families; in respectful relationships between bosses and employees; in wealth and power generously put at the service of the weak. Sometimes, to see greatness, it's better to look down rather than up.

God of justice, give me the courage to speak
and act for the small and the voiceless.

PAUSE AND CONSIDER: What makes a person great? A nation great? How does the cross of Jesus redefine greatness?

Open-door Policy

If we have died with Christ, we believe that we
shall also live with him. ROMANS 6:8

Most of us don't feel anxious about our loved ones who made it into heaven by a wide margin. We may feel sure our grandmother, as well as the friend who was close to the church, enjoys the presence of God. Doubt may set in about the baby who died unbaptized; the relative who was a fallen-away Catholic; or the neighbor who died by suicide. Did they die without Christ? Is there still a chance they might live with him?

What does the church teach about the citizens of heaven? It says some people are certainly in heaven, like those on the rolls of the canonized saints. Interestingly, the church has never insisted that any one particular person is in hell or even in purgatory. God's mercy is wide. Our knowledge of another person's soul is always uncertain. We can presume the door to salvation is, therefore, open. That's why we pray for the dead: there's always room for hope.

Compassionate God, you're nowhere near
as prepared to condemn us as we are.

PAUSE AND CONSIDER: How do you honor the dead, keep them in holy memory, and intercede for them in prayer?

Sweet Dreams

"This is the will of the one who sent me, that I should not lose anything of what he gave me." JOHN 6:39

Sometimes we dream of those who have died. They may seem happy and at peace, which may be a sign of consolation for us. Or they may seem preoccupied with some task set before them, or troubled in some way. That could be a sign that they're in need of our prayers. In the Bible, the world of dreams is understood as a realm of communication between the realities of the spirit and the flesh. There's no reason to believe this has changed.

Can we receive news from our loved ones who have died? Many people seem to get such messages, in dreams or in signs that have meaning only for them. A bird out of season lights on the bush a deceased husband planted. A stranger uses an odd parting phrase that a friend was famous for. Are these winks from heaven, assurances that even when we lose our dear ones, nothing is really lost?

Lord, thank you for the rich communion enjoyed between us and those who've gone before us.

PAUSE AND CONSIDER: "Burying the dead" is one of the corporal works of mercy. It includes all the ways we honor our deceased, including remembering them in our Eucharist, holding them in prayer, and being grateful for how they live on in us.

Bridge over Troubled Water

"The winding roads shall be made straight, and the rough ways made smooth." LUKE 3:5

The day I was fired by an impossible-to-please boss, I didn't know whether to laugh or cry. My time on the job had been miserable. Still, a job's a job; not having one is generally worse than having a difficult one. I was prepared to spend the evening feeling sorry for myself. But my now-former coworker Cindy suggested another course of action: "Let's have a sad party."

A sad party? How do you celebrate loss? But celebrate we did. We dressed up like two kids invading mom's closet, down to the garish lipstick and cloppy high heels. We went to a karaoke club and sang torch songs like divas. And yes, I was still just as fired as I had been a few hours earlier. I still had to face the want ads the next morning. But the anger, frustration, and disappointment lifted like a cloud. Having a friend like Cindy made the rough way smooth.

God of consolation, thank you for the friends
I have. Help me be a good friend to others.

PAUSE AND CONSIDER: Don't permit the circumstances of a passing world to crush the hope that is yours in Christ. Pray for courage. Form community. Be a friend to someone who needs one.

What Should We Do?

[God] will sing joyfully because of you, as on festival days. ZEPHANIAH 3:17–18

The prophet says something really wonderful here: God wants to sing a love song to you. No kidding. God is like the lover who croons in your ear the melody you share together, your special song, so you always remember how unique the love you share is. Images like this from the Bible may confound us. We don't know what to make of this kind of love from God. We're deeply moved when another person loves us this way. But God? How do we accept being cherished by the Creator of the universe?

Yet we should, because we are. Since God delights in us this way, no wonder Zephaniah recommends we shout for joy and sing too. It doesn't matter if your voice is only good enough for the shower. Happy people stroll around with a song in their hearts. They should know we are Christians by our humming.

Lord of love and song, how glad I am to be so beloved.

PAUSE AND CONSIDER: How do you feel about the love God has for you: embarrassed, grateful, shocked, disbelieving? How do you return such love?

Today Is Holy

"Go, eat rich foods and drink sweet drinks … ;
for today is holy to our LORD." NEHEMIAH 8:10

Here's a prophecy we can all appreciate: Eat, drink, and be merry! Now that's a celebration fit for a holy day. Ezra the priest gave this advice because the people were weeping and causing a general state of despair. How did this mass depression come about? After a generation in exile, the citizens of Jerusalem returned home. They rebuilt the destroyed temple and reclaimed the teachings of Moses. The rediscovered scroll of those teachings was read aloud in the assembly. Suddenly the community was conscience-stricken to recognize how poorly they'd kept faith with God. Shame led to wailing. Ezra urged them to party instead.

His point was simple. Yes, the people had sinned, but God is compassionate. Rejoicing would demonstrate their confidence in divine mercy. Tears only bore witness to their fear of God's wrath. A lot of us spend too much time mourning God's judgment and too little time celebrating God's forgiveness.

Compassionate God, you know what I've done and failed to do. Yet you forgive!

PAUSE AND CONSIDER: How can you celebrate the holiness of this day, and every day, blessed by the mercy of God?

The Thing about Enemies

"Love your enemies, do good to those who hate you, bless those who curse you, pray for those who mistreat you." LUKE 6:27–28

We already know what happens when we hurt people who hurt us or say nasty things to someone who's just said mean words to us. Violence begets more violence, and bad feelings generate more bad feelings. History tells this story so often it starts to sound silly that some people still believe it can end differently than it always does.

But consider the offbeat chance that some of us might take Jesus seriously when he says to answer evil with good, love your enemies, reply to curses with kindness. What kind of a world might emerge from those choices? Could our enemies remain enemies if the only response they got from us was kindness, generosity, care, and blessings? Wouldn't it be wonderful to live in a world where we might learn the answer to that question? Maybe Jesus just doesn't understand the complexity of the issues. But I suspect he does.

Loving God, receiving an enemy without enmity feels impossible. Give me the grace to do it.

PAUSE AND CONSIDER: Next time you see the "enemy"—the woman you argue with, the child who irritates you, the man who inspires anger—change tactics. Choose an open way to encounter that person.

Once More with Feeling

Whoever is in Christ is a new creation:
the old things have passed away; behold, new
things have come. 2 CORINTHIANS 5:17

Newness is often something to celebrate. It could be a new year, birthday, or baby; a new car, address, job, or simply a hairstyle. Embracing the new gives us a surge of hope that change is possible. The clock is still ticking. We have another chance to get it right. There's time to become the people we dream of being. Though the past can threaten with its disappointments and failures, the arrival of something new hints that the future still harbors some surprises.

So, try the new diet; make Lenten resolutions; join the support group; quit the deadening job; dare to bring children into the world; invest in a new friendship. Though relationships have gone awry, we can still hope to restore peace. Though we've not been very good at following the law of love as Jesus taught us, love is still a choice we can make—today and tonight and tomorrow.

I want to be a new creation! You who created
the original model, lead me to wholeness.

PAUSE AND CONSIDER: What's old and stale and dead in your life? Where's the growing, hopeful edge that might lead you to a better tomorrow?

Let Heaven and Nature Sing

Then I heard every creature in heaven and on earth,…
everything in the universe, cry out. REVELATION 5:13

The ancients speculated that angel-song kept the celestial spheres in balance and harmony. Perhaps our inability to hear such music keeps us crashing into one another. In John's vision, we hear of a time beyond time when all creation will be united in praise of God. Can you imagine heaven and earth, human and beast, maybe even the stones, united in a spirit of reverence? One Lord created us. One day Christ will be "all in all." If unity isn't our intention, we're in for some bad times.

Don't you feel a bit of kinship with the natural world when you walk through a forest or sit by the ocean? Doesn't it seem certain that your dog knows your heart? Even that strange craze of pet rocks begins to make sense. As Saint Francis says, Brother Sun and Sister Moon are part of the family God created. Join the song!

God of everything, keep me mindful
of my place within creation.

PAUSE AND CONSIDER: How do you experience kinship with the natural world? How does this kinship make stewardship of earth a matter of urgency?

Yours, Mine, and Ours

There are different kinds of spiritual gifts
but the same Spirit. 1 CORINTHIANS 12:4

At Christmastime, families often sit together by the tree to open their presents. Does everyone receive the same-shaped box with an identical gift waiting inside? No, but this inequality doesn't mean some are more loved than others. Rita gets a 2,000-piece jigsaw puzzle, which would be a form of death to Mark—yet Rita could not be happier. Mark gets a collection of vintage vinyl records that sound like wails from the seventh level of hell to Rita—but Mark is beside himself with excitement. Each gets the appropriate gift—not the same, but just right.

Each of us is called and shaped by our experiences for a life of holiness. Each is as far from a cookie-cutter saint as possible. Yet all are given what we need to shine by the God who loves us equally. Identify your gifts and celebrate them. Not one of us is left wanting by the Spirit's generosity.

Thank you, generous God, for the things I can do that give me delight and fulfillment.

PAUSE AND CONSIDER: Consider what you're good at, as well as the complementary gifts of your inner circle. How can these attributes serve the one Lord?

Tell What You Know

"You will receive power when the holy Spirit comes upon you, and you will be my witnesses… to the ends of the earth." ACTS OF THE APOSTLES 1:8

Witnessing to the ends of the earth sounds like hard work. Some days I don't feel up to witnessing across the breakfast table. But a key part of Jesus' commission is that the power of the Spirit makes this evangelizing mission possible. If it were strictly up to you and me, Christianity would hardly make it down the block.

However, the vital role of the Spirit in this enterprise doesn't mean we get to relax in our rocking chairs and watch the gospel spread to the ends of the earth on television. The Spirit dwells in us. It moves in

A LITTLE BOOK OF LIGHT

concert with our efforts. It's like those stories Jesus always tells: even though the yield of the soil to one hundredfold comes from God, the sower still has to get off the recliner and plant the seed. We do our little part so the Spirit can multiply it. It's the best matching grant in the universe!

Lord, take me in hand and plant my efforts where they are most needed.

PAUSE AND CONSIDER: How can you witness to the love of God with your words, example, money, time, presence, vote, and service?

Wisdom Starts Here

Thus says Wisdom: "When [the LORD] established the heavens, there was I." **PROVERBS 8:27**

The wisest person I ever met was a cloistered nun in a monastery in Texas. Our paths crossed at a time when I felt truly lost. I had been held at knifepoint on the way home from a vigil for peace. The experience brought me close to death for the longest 15 minutes of my life. Though I was rescued and survived, afterward I fell into a depression. Something about praying for peace and falling victim to violence wounded me in a place I didn't know how to heal.

I went to the monastery in search of my lost peace. The spiritual director assigned to me didn't try to talk me back from despair. Instead, each day she gave me a single line of Scripture to contemplate. I devoured each word like a starving person. I begged God to graft them onto my soul. Thanks to that wise nun, light dawned in my heart again like a new creation.

Lord, raise up the wise in every corner of the world, so that we might share their light.

PAUSE AND CONSIDER: When have you encountered wisdom in a personal exchange, a book, a story, or an event? How does the encounter with wisdom change you?

Tangible Mysteries

The Lord Jesus took bread, broke it and said,
"This is my body that is for you." 1 CORINTHIANS 11:23-24

The teaching Paul hands on to his community is as tangible as bread and wine. This is a priceless aspect of our sacrament: you can hold it in your hand, touch and taste and see it. Far from an abstract idea of grace, it's a divine truth as incarnate as you are. When all the theology you've ever heard starts to sound like a head trip, here's a manifestation of God you can cup your hand around!

It was unlikely that first generation of disciples would ever forget the experience of being in the presence of Jesus. Even his Ascension couldn't take that away from them. Jesus establishes his everlasting table for the generations to come. How would we keep him in vital memory? How would the Body of Christ be real for us when that body is so long ago ascended? Hold out your hand and touch the mystery.

Your food feeds the hungry world.
Your cup rescues those close to death.

PAUSE AND CONSIDER: Every shared meal is sacred insofar as it gives life. Share your food with the hungry. Be a guardian of clean water for all.

Let's Make a Deal

"For everyone who asks, receives; ... and to the one who
knocks, the door will be opened." LUKE 11:10

There are two schools of thought about making deals with God. One:
it's a terrible idea, a misuse of the relationship, and just plain silly.
The other: it's done all the time in the Bible. Abraham dickers with
strangers who plan to destroy two cities. Moses tries to talk God down
from wiping out the Israelites and starting over with a more compliant
nation. David fasts and prays to win back the life of his dying son. One
out of three is successful in bargaining with God. Are these good odds?

Jesus encourages us to approach God persistently for what we need.
Like Abraham and David, we have to accept the final answer when it
comes. But making our needs, desires, and hopes known to God is our
right. We call this activity the prayer of petition. Not to ask is not to
trust. Every honest relationship begins with taking risks.

In a world full of closed doors, Lord, give me
big fists, a loud voice, and a stout heart.

PAUSE AND CONSIDER: Practice the prayer of petition daily. Get comfortable with putting every desire of your heart before the God who
can be trusted.

Check Your Closets

"Teacher, tell my brother to share the inheritance with me." LUKE 12:13

Someone near Jesus is worried about getting a fair share of the inheritance. I bet some of us are too. I know someone who's been planning
how to spend her inheritance since high school—and her parents are

alive and well. We live out of the shallowest one percent of ourselves when we allow mere stuff to become the driving force of our energies.

Consider how much time you spend on money: getting it, spending it, worrying about it, managing it. Is this a balanced use of your time? Jesus tells a story of a rich man whose barn is too small to hold the harvest he hasn't even planted yet. We know folks convinced they need a bigger house, another car, a storage space downtown. It seems silly to mention that maybe what they need is less stuff. If you run out of hangers for your clothes, the last thing you need is more hangers.

Lord, my life is stuffed with things, activities, expectations. Please empty my barn!

PAUSE AND CONSIDER: Make a little room in your closets. Give stuff to people who could use it. Empty out your schedule. Make space for prayer, silence, and peace.

Words Become Flesh

Take as your norm the sound words that you heard from me… in Christ Jesus. 2 TIMOTHY 1:13

Whose words have influenced your life the most? Maybe it was something your parents or a beloved teacher or mentor said. Perhaps you read a book that inspired you or followed the career of someone whose accomplishments motivated you. My older sister was inspired by my mother's patient and gentle parenting to become that kind of parent herself. Another sister chose to model her life on the words of Thérèse of Lisieux; she became a Third Order Carmelite. Me? I was captivated by the works of Sir Arthur Conan Doyle and his sharp-thinking, dry-witted detective Sherlock Holmes. Eventually, I connected the dots between Holmes' analytical consideration of criminal mysteries and the greater pursuit of mysteries through theology and Scripture. No matter whose words originally move us to act, it's inescapable that words affect us. Even violent words thrown our way may compel us to act in defiance of them and become people of peace.

God whose words created a world and became flesh, teach me to treat words with reverence.

PAUSE AND CONSIDER: Consider the words you live by: slogans, famous quotes, or verses from Scripture that speak to you profoundly. How might your words be affecting those around you?

Good Trouble

*And a widow in that town used to come
to [the judge] and say, "Render a just decision
for me against my adversary."* LUKE 18:3

The Parable of the Importunate Widow, as it's traditionally called, is unfortunately named. The unfamiliar word "importunate" simply means "troublemaker." Imagine that: the judge isn't called a troublemaker for being unjust, but the woman is considered a nuisance because she demands justice! This skewed perspective is common in our world. Environmentalists, peacemakers, and justice seekers are seen as problematic people for preferring a world with water and trees and without racism, poverty, and war. Life advocates are troublemakers for wanting to protect the right to life in the womb, the nursing home, the hospital, and even the penitentiary. People who won't stand for gender exclusivity, economic oppression, and the omission of anyone's voice from the corridors of power are labeled "the problem" instead of "the solution." As Representative John Lewis always said, we need more people willing to become holy nuisances and to cause this "good kind of trouble."

*God of justice and mercy, deepen my commitment
to a society that works for all its members.*

PAUSE AND CONSIDER: Choose one justice issue you feel strongly about (inequality, peace, climate change, right to life, health care, etc.) and deepen your dedication through prayer, study, and action.

Speak the Fire!

*There appeared to them tongues as of fire,
which parted and came to rest on each one of them.* **ACTS OF THE APOSTLES 2:3**

I like the description of the Pentecost event as a visitation of "tongues." This idea appears twice in the story: first as flames that settle on each person present in the upper room and next as a miraculous language spoken in the streets and understood by all. Tongues are for talking: it makes sense that the first gift gave rise to the second.

I want to believe such language is still available to us in the church. No, I don't mean charismatic speech; Saint Paul describes the limited usefulness of speaking a language discernible to just a few. The gift we really need are tongues readily understood by everybody: those who speak my language and those who don't. It's for folks in the global South as well as the global North. For those who've been loved and those only despised. Where's the language that speaks to conservatives and liberals, believers and atheists? It's a language we all must learn.

*Spirit of understanding, ignite my compassion
to soften my words so they communicate.*

PAUSE AND CONSIDER: Who do you know who's learned how to speak across gaps: generations, ideologies, cultures, life experiences? How can you emulate that gift?

Give Peace a Chance

The warrior's bow will be banished,
and [your king] will proclaim peace to
the nations. ZECHARIAH 9:10

Bullies don't believe the world will respect them if they stop punching. So, they keep on punching. To them, it's either hit or be hit. Most bullies learned this equation the hard way, on the opposite end of the fist.

But just because you've memorized a lesson doesn't make it true. Is aggression the only route to strength, dignity, and power? Most foreign policies and business strategies would say yes. The man on the cross says no. The man on the cross says strength is revealed in vulnerability, dignity in humiliation, and power in the emptying of privilege. Is the man on the cross crazy, or is the world crazy?

Bullies keep on punching because they're afraid to stop. Foreign policies continue to rely on guns and bombs. Businesses don't hesitate to cheat to get their market share. Those who follow the man on the cross will think twice about these things.

Source of all peace, teach us that justice
is the only way to genuine peace.

PAUSE AND CONSIDER: When have I used my authority like a bully? Do I bully myself internally? Who feels or fears the power of my fists and words?

I Am with You Always

"And behold, I am with you always, until the end of the age." MATTHEW 28:20

When I was a child, it seemed the point of the Ascension story was that Jesus LEFT. In a nutshell: he was here, then he died, then he rose, and then he went "home." The Ascension is the divine curtain call. Apparently, Jesus has to be removed for the church to take over. An awkward side effect of resurrection is that he has to be ushered from view a second time. Ascension provided a method of extraction sufficiently dramatic to make it work with the rest of the story. You can't just have him walk down the road into the sunset!

This theory has one great flaw: Jesus makes the exact opposite point in his final words in Matthew's gospel. Jesus doesn't say, "Bye for now, see you later, beam me up!" He says, "I am (*present tense*) with you (*staying right here*) always (*a long-term proposition*)." Jesus is HERE— unless the age ended while we weren't looking.

God of comings and goings, keep an eye on me in my ups and downs.

PAUSE AND CONSIDER: Celebrate Ascension with everything that goes up: sunrise, birds, birthdays, balloons. Celebrate Ascension with what endures: love, fidelity, friendship, church.